JANE AUSTEN
and her world

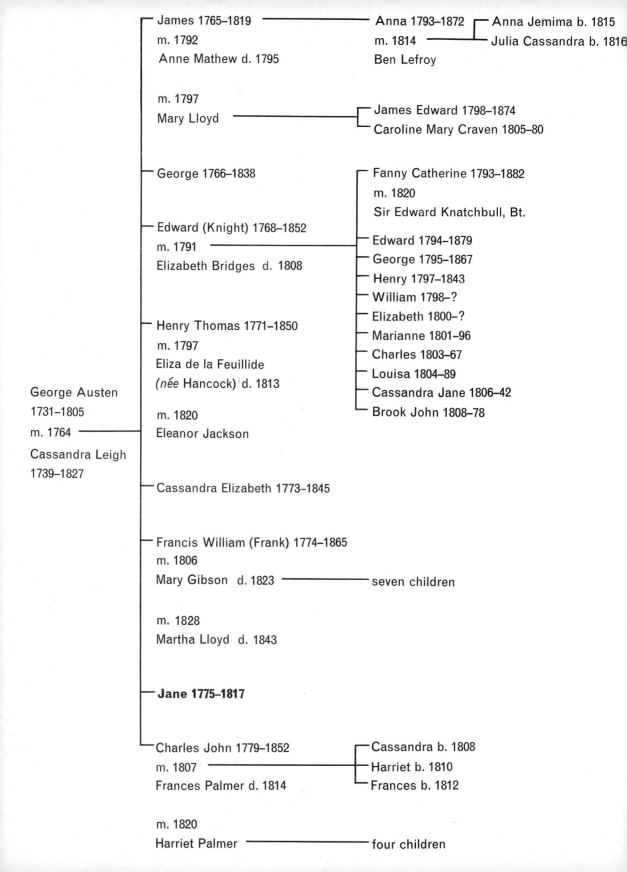

James 1765–1819
m. 1792
Anne Mathew d. 1795

Anna 1793–1872
m. 1814
Ben Lefroy

Anna Jemima b. 1815
Julia Cassandra b. 1816

m. 1797
Mary Lloyd

James Edward 1798–1874
Caroline Mary Craven 1805–80

George 1766–1838

Edward (Knight) 1768–1852
m. 1791
Elizabeth Bridges d. 1808

Fanny Catherine 1793–1882
m. 1820
Sir Edward Knatchbull, Bt.

Edward 1794–1879
George 1795–1867
Henry 1797–1843
William 1798–?
Elizabeth 1800–?
Marianne 1801–96
Charles 1803–67
Louisa 1804–89
Cassandra Jane 1806–42
Brook John 1808–78

Henry Thomas 1771–1850
m. 1797
Eliza de la Feuillide
(née Hancock) d. 1813

m. 1820
Eleanor Jackson

George Austen
1731–1805
m. 1764
Cassandra Leigh
1739–1827

Cassandra Elizabeth 1773–1845

Francis William (Frank) 1774–1865
m. 1806
Mary Gibson d. 1823 ——— seven children

m. 1828
Martha Lloyd d. 1843

Jane 1775–1817

Charles John 1779–1852
m. 1807
Frances Palmer d. 1814

Cassandra b. 1808
Harriet b. 1810
Frances b. 1812

m. 1820
Harriet Palmer ——————— four children

JANE AUSTEN

and her world

BY MARGHANITA LASKI

 THAMES AND HUDSON · LONDON

To Elizabeth Jenkins

Printed in Great Britain by Jarrold & Sons Ltd, Norwich

500 13023 X

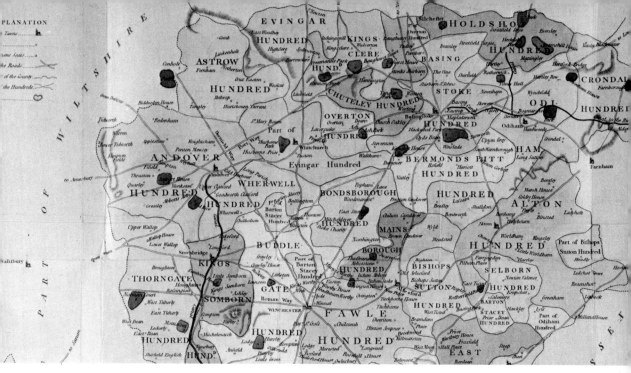

Hampshire in 1791; Steventon is in the south-west of Basingstoke Hundred

IN 1870, EDWARD AUSTEN-LEIGH, then Vicar of Bray, published a
Memoir of his aunt Jane Austen. In the years between her death in 1817 and this
publication there had been no public interest in her life and little in her works.
Only one collected edition of her novels had been published, in 1833, and this
in a popular series which included much now-forgotten trivia. Certainly a few
people throughout this period greatly enjoyed Jane Austen's works, but their
attempts to share their enjoyment often failed. John Henry Newman, still a
Protestant clergyman, wrote in 1837, 'Miss Austen has no romance – none at all.
What vile creatures her parsons are!', and sharp-tongued Mrs Carlyle in 1843, of
'Miss Austen': 'Too washy; water-gruel for mind and body at the same time were
too bad.' Charlotte Brontë could not enter into Mrs Gaskell's enthusiasm for
Jane Austen; in 1850, Charlotte Brontë wrote to another equally enthusiastic
friend,

> Her business is not half so much with the human heart as with the human eyes,
> mouth, hands, and feet. What sees keenly, speaks aptly, moves flexibly, it suits
> her to study; but what throbs fast and full, though hidden, what the blood
> rushes through, what is the unseen seat of life and the sentient target of death –
> this Miss Austen ignores. . . . Jane Austen was a complete and most sensible
> lady, but a very incomplete and rather insensible (*not senseless*) woman. If this
> is heresy, I cannot help it.

5

But among those who liked Jane Austen's work, some gave it the highest praise. It was Archbishop Whately in 1821 who first compared her with Shakespeare, and the same comparison was made by Macaulay in 1843 in respect of her powers of caricature, and by G. H. Lewes in 1847, referring to her 'marvellous dramatic power'. Tennyson put her 'next to Shakespeare', and, in about 1860, 'thanked God Almighty with his whole heart that he knew nothing, and that the world knew nothing of Jane Austen, and that there were no letters preserved either of Shakespeare's or of Jane Austen's, that they had not been ripped open like pigs.'

Some ten years later Edward Austen-Leigh's Memoir appeared, and to a large extent Tennyson's thankfulness had become invalid. Jane Austen had been a copious letter writer, especially to her sister Cassandra. Apart from some discreet excisions by Cassandra, these letters have largely been preserved and from 1870 onwards were being published. Thanks to them, thanks to the Memoir and to later family reminiscences, thanks to the researches both of scholars and of amateurs, we now probably know as much of the social life of Jane Austen among her family and friends as of any author who ever lived.

But in another respect Tennyson's ghost may still offer thanks. Of the creative and emotional life of Jane Austen we know almost nothing. The kind of self-revelations her contemporary Wordsworth was making in *The Prelude*, the kind of connections we can fairly make between Keats's poems and the self-exposures of the letters he was writing when Jane Austen died, are in her case almost entirely lacking. 'To strangers,' wrote her niece Caroline Austen in 1867, 'they [*sc.* the letters] could be *no* transcript of her mind – they would not feel they knew her any the better for having read them.' So far as knowing the creative and emotional life of Jane Austen is concerned, her niece was right. What the letters and the other evidence give us is the fully documented life of a family of small country gentry at the turn of the last century, a documentation we owe to the fact that one of its members was a writer who became famous.

Jane Austen's Father So far as social standing goes, that of George Austen, Jane Austen's father, was a little inferior to his wife's. His was an old Kentish family, in the Middle Ages members of that group of clothiers known as the Grey Coats of Kent. By the sixteenth century the family had acquired two small manor houses, Grovehurst and Broadford, and in the next two centuries some members had become substantial landowners. But George Austen's branch was poor. His grandmother, left a young widow with five sons and a daughter, had moved to Sevenoaks so that her sons might have a good classical education at the grammar school there. The fourth of these sons, William, was George Austen's father.

William Austen was a surgeon at Tonbridge, at a period when medical men did not rank highly in the middle-class social scale. He married a widow, Rebecca

Thomas Babington Macaulay

Alfred Lord Tennyson

The Rev. George Austen (1731–1805), 'the handsome Proctor'

Francis Austen of Sevenoaks, George Austen's uncle and benefactor

Walter, with a son, William Hampson Walter, and of his own many children two survived, a daughter Philadelphia, and George who was born in 1731.

Both of George Austen's parents died when he was young, and a rich uncle, Francis Austen, stepped in to help the children. Philadelphia was shipped to Madras in 1752 and there, the next year, she married Tysoe Saul Hancock, the surgeon at Fort St David. George was sent to Tonbridge School, then to St John's College, Oxford, where he gained an Open Scholarship. He left Oxford to teach at his old school and in 1758 he was Second Master there, but the next year he was back in Oxford as a Fellow of St John's. He was known as 'the handsome

Left, Tonbridge School, where George Austen was educated

Left below, Walcot Church, Bath. Here George Austen married Cassandra Leigh in 1764 and was buried in 1805

Right, an attack by Hogarth on Pope's *Epistle of Taste*. A is Pope and B the first Duke of Chandos, Jane Austen's maternal great-uncle by marriage

proctor', and handsome, by all reports, he was, with prematurely white curly hair and exceptionally bright hazel eyes. In 1760 he took orders, and in 1764 he married Cassandra Leigh at Walcot Church in Bath.

Her family was as old as his own and socially more elevated. One ancestor, Sir Thomas Leigh, had been Lord Mayor of London under Queen Elizabeth. His son, in 1642, had sheltered Charles I, at Stoneleigh Abbey in Warwickshire, the family seat of the younger, ennobled branch of the family, the Leighs of Adlestrop in Gloucestershire, to which Cassandra belonged. Her grandfather was a Brydges, brother-in-law to that Duke of Chandos whose ostentatious display of wealth was satirized by Pope. Her father, elected a Fellow of All Souls so young that he was known as 'Chick Leigh', became Rector of Harpsden, near Henley-on-Thames, where Cassandra was brought up.

Her Mother

She, like her husband, was good-looking, with a noble nose of which she was proud. It is said that she might have been known as 'the beautiful Miss Leigh' had that title not belonged to her sister Jane who had married Dr Edward Cooper, the Rector of Whaddon near Bath.

9

Ashe Rectory, the home of the Rev. Isaac Lefroy (1745–1806) and his wife 'Madam' Lefroy (1749–1804)

Below, Deane House near Steventon, the home of the Austens' friends, the Harwoods

By the time that George Austen married Cassandra Leigh, he was, thanks to the good offices of his relations, comfortably able to support a wife. In addition to rich Uncle Francis, he had a well-disposed and well-endowed kinsman in Thomas Knight, a substantial landowner both in Kent, where his seat was Godmersham House, and in Hampshire where he owned Chawton Manor House, near Alton, and other property. The living of Steventon, just off the Basingstoke–Andover road, was in his gift and this, in 1761, he presented to his second cousin George. Moreover, Francis Austen, doubtful whether this benefice would be substantial enough, bought the livings of two near-by parishes, Deane and Ashe, intending to give George whichever first fell vacant; this proved, in the event, to be Deane.

There is no evidence that George Austen had resided at Steventon before his marriage in 1764. Family tradition had it that he and his wife had first settled at Deane, removing to Steventon in 1771, with Mrs Austen perched on a pile of

Steventon

Front view of Steventon Rectory, drawn by Jane Austen's niece, Anna Lefroy

Godmersham Park,
Kent, the seat of
Thomas Knight,
Edward Austen's
adoptive father

The Hampshire
countryside in the late
eighteenth century

mattresses on a cart against the jolting of the ill-made country lanes. It now seems almost certain that they returned directly from their wedding journey to Steventon Rectory, and that it was at Steventon, in 1765, that their first son, James, was born.

Brothers and Sisters

James, or Jemmy, as his parents called him in childhood, was followed in 1766 by George, about whom we know almost nothing. A letter of Mrs Austen's in 1770 tells of 'my poor little George' being brought to see her, and of the frustrated hopes that he might have no more fits. Apart from this, no reference to him appears in family correspondence or recollections, beyond a bare announcement of his death in 1838. Jane Austen refers, in 1808, to being able to talk to the deaf with her fingers, and this may give a clue to some part of poor George's condition.

Edward was born in 1768, Henry Thomas in 1771, and the first girl, Cassandra Elizabeth, in 1773. Then in 1774 came Francis William, known in the family as Frank, in 1775 Jane and in 1779 the last child, Charles John.

Jane Austen's Birth

Jane's birthday was 16 December. Her godparents were Uncle Francis's wife Jane, a Mrs Musgrove who was a connection of her mother's, and the Reverend Samuel Cooke who had married Mrs Austen's cousin, another Cassandra Leigh, the daughter of the Reverend Theophilus Leigh, Master of Balliol College, Oxford.

Mrs Austen kept up a warm correspondence with Mrs Walter, the wife of George Austen's half-brother, and inevitably many letters were about the children. These had been, as was then not uncommon, put out to nurse for their first year or so, in the neighbouring village of Deane. No neglect was implied by this. They were visited constantly by their parents, and the separation was probably no greater than it would have been by dismissal to a Victorian or Edwardian nursery. When Cassandra came back from nurse, Mrs Austen wrote to her sister-in-law, 'I want to show you my Henry and my Cassy, who are both reckoned very fine children,' and soon after, of Cassy, 'My little girl talks all day long, and, in my opinion, is a very entertaining companion.' When Francis was born, she was able to say that he was 'very stout' – that is, sturdy, but it was left to Mr Austen to report the birth of Jane, the day after the event. He wrote, 'She is to be Jenny, and seems to me as if she would be as like Henry as Cassy is to Neddy.' He was speaking, of course, of physical likenesses: Edward and Cassy had black eyes and their mother's aquiline nose, whereas Henry, alone among the children, had inherited his father's bright hazel eyes, and Jane something of the kind, though less startling. But the affinities extended beyond the physical: Edward was to be Cassandra's favourite brother, and Henry, Jane's.

The children had been born to happy, talented parents and to a pleasant home. Steventon Rectory was pulled down in 1826, but from family reminiscences and sketches we have a good idea what it was like after George Austen had made his improvements to the 'cottage' he found when he went there.

Above, Mrs George Austen, *née* Cassandra Leigh (1739–1827)

Left, James Austen (1765–1819), George Austen's eldest son

Steventon lies in the pleasant, well-wooded, undramatic chalk country of northern Hampshire. The Rectory or Parsonage House (it is variously referred to) was at the end of a street of cottages, a two-storied house with dormer attic windows, a carriage drive to the north, a garden to the south with a turfed terrace down which the child Jane Austen was said, like her own Catherine Morland, to be fond of rolling; two extended hedgerows, one sheltered by fine old elms, formed shrubbery walks from the garden, and facing the house, on the other side of the lane, was a large barn that played a great part in family entertainments.

From the trellised porch the front door opened into the family parlour. At the front, too, was the dining-room, at the back the Rector's bow-windowed study. We do not know what Mr Austen's income was, but when he retired he anticipated having £600 p.a., and this, presumably, after paying two curates. At Steventon it was sufficient to maintain a carriage and horses, though these, like Mr Bennet's

of *Pride and Prejudice*, were probably called out for farm use when need arose. His own and his wife's tastes were simple. Mrs Austen had been to London once or twice, notably to help Mrs Walter through a confinement, but came back saying, ''Tis a sad place. I would not live in it on any account, one has not time to do one's duty either to God or to man.' She had no use for ostentation. When she married she had owned a scarlet riding habit, and this she wore around her household tasks until it was at last cut up to make a little suit for Francis when he was first breeched; and visitors were apt to find Mrs Austen busy with her domestic mending in the front parlour, to the embarrassment of her daughters. Probably she, like Mrs Morland of *Northanger Abbey*, gave her little girls their first education; and with her children, her dairy (the Austens kept five Alderney cows), overseeing the baking of the household bread and the brewing of the household beer, she was fully occupied.

16

◀ A plain coach of about 1750. 'You have a nice day for your Journey in whatever way it is to be performed – whether in the Debary's Coach or on your own twenty toes.' (*Letter* from JA to Cassandra, 21 May 1801)

Mrs Hancock, *née* Philadelphia Austen, George Austen's sister

Whatever his income, Mr Austen augmented it by taking resident pupils, 'a few youths of chosen friends and acquaintances.' The first of these came to him through the good offices of his sister Philadelphia. In India she had become friendly with a Mrs Buchanan, an officer's widow, who married Warren Hastings. In 1759 Mrs Hastings died in childbirth, leaving a delicate three-year-old son George who, on Philadelphia Hancock's recommendation, was later sent home to the charge of her brother George Austen and his wife. This child, who probably accompanied the Austens on their wedding journey, died at the age of six from the then common killer, a 'putrid sore throat'. Warren Hastings, however, remained perpetually grateful to the Austens and the Hancocks for their care of his son, and in 1761, when Philadelphia's daughter Eliza (or Betsy, as she was first known) was born at Calcutta, he stood godfather to her and gave £10,000 in trust for her parents and her.

Mr Austen's Pupils

17

Little George Hastings had died too young to play any part in the Austen family life but there were other pupils. Lord Lymington, the eldest son of Lord Portsmouth, came in 1773, when he was six; when he was grown up he was to invite the Austen girls to the annual ball at Hurstbourne Park. Master Vander-stegen came the same year; he was nearly fourteen and backward, but 'very good tempered and well-disposed'. Then in 1779 there was Thomas Craven Fowle, of whom we shall hear more.

The Knights   By the time that Jane was entering childhood, the family population was necessarily a shifting one. Edward had already left home for good. Rich, childless Thomas Knight, the son of George Austen's benefactor, had asked that the boy should visit him and his wife in Kent. Mr Austen had demurred, fearing impair-ment of studies, but Mrs Austen providently said, 'I think, my dear, you had better oblige your cousins and let the child go,' and when the Knights asked to adopt the boy and bring him up as their heir, the Austens agreed. So Edward was brought up at Godmersham Park as heir to a great estate, and, at the proper time, sent not to university but to make the Grand Tour on the Continent.

The trial of Warren Hastings, which opened in Westminster Hall in February, 1788. He was godfather to George Austen's niece, Eliza Hancock

Hurstbourne Park, seat of Lord Portsmouth whose heir, Viscount Lymington, was a pupil at Steventon Rectory

The Rev. George Austen presents his son Edward to Mr and Mrs Thomas Knight

Mr Thomas Knight of Godmersham, by George Romney
Mrs Thomas Knight (*née* Catherine Knatchbull), by George Romney

20

A young gentleman on the Grand Tour is benevolent to French beggars

One of the rooms in the Musée des Monuments, Paris, c. 1800; a young gentleman who took
the Grand Tour, as Edward Austen did, would be expected to visit such instructive sights as this

The Knights had made the right choice for their purposes, for Edward was the sensible, solid, practical son. Mrs Austen, comparing Edward and James in later years, wrote that Edward was 'quite a man of business. That my dear James was not. Classical knowledge, literary taste, and the power of elegant composition he possessed in the highest degree. *Both* equally good, amiable and sweet-tempered.'

The scholarly James, the eldest son, went up to Oxford to his father's old college, St John's, but as Founder's Kin, from his mother's connections. Here he visited his mother's formidable uncle, Theophilus Leigh of Balliol, a noted wit and punster, who disconcerted the young man when he first came to dinner and ignorantly took off his gown, by saying, 'Young man, you need not strip; we are not going to fight.'

Henry, Jane Austen's favourite brother and a substantial influence in her life, was undoubtedly handsome and charming, but some people were apt to look on his other talents with a less universally approving eye than Jane and her father cast on him. James's daughter Anna was to write, and probably justly:

He was the handsomest of the family, and in the opinion of his father, the most talented. There were others who formed a different opinion, but, for the most

◄ St John's College, Oxford.
George Austen and his sons
James and Henry were all
Scholars there

Henry Thomas Austen
(1771–1850), painted after 1816
when he took Orders

part, he was greatly admired. Brilliant in conversation he was, and, like his father, blessed with a hopefulness of temper which, in adapting itself to all circumstances, served to create a perpetual sunshine.

In 1782, Cassandra and Jane, together with their cousin Jane Cooper, were sent away to school. It had been Mrs Austen's intention to send only Cassandra, thinking Jane, at seven, too young to go away. But 'If Cassandra were going to have her head cut off, Jane would insist on sharing her fate,' said Mrs Austen, and the little girls went off together to Oxford, to Mrs Cawley who was Dr Cooper's sister and the widow of a Principal of Brasenose College. *Schooldays*

The next year Mrs Cawley removed her small establishment to Southampton, and there the dreaded 'putrid sore throat' struck the school. Mrs Cawley did not inform the parents, but young Jane Cooper wrote to her mother who, with her sister Mrs Austen, came post-haste to take the little girls away. Unfortunately it was Mrs Cooper who caught the putrid throat and died of it.

The second and last school to which the three girls were sent was the Abbey School at Reading, in the gatehouse of the old Abbey. Kept by an elderly Mrs Latournelle it seems to have been a model of kindliness and casualness.

23

Mrs Sherwood, author of *The Fairchild Family*, also attended the Abbey School, and has left a fairly full account of it. So long, it appears, as the girls attended their tutor in his study for an hour or two each morning, no one asked where they were the rest of the day between meals; when Edward Austen and Edward Cooper and some other young men called at the Abbey School, they were allowed to take their young sisters out to dinner at a local inn.

For whatever education the girls were scrambled into at the Abbey School Mr Austen paid something under £40 a year. It seems likely that a more useful education was acquired at home where they returned in 1786 or 1787. Their father was a substantial classical scholar with an excellent library, and no check seems to have been placed on the girls' reading, or on conversation either. Since the popular picture of Jane Austen was formed in later Victorian times, after the publication of Edward Austen-Leigh's Memoir, it is important to remember that she was in fact a Georgian and brought up in the frank atmosphere of that enlightened age, an atmosphere in no way incompatible with the sincere if unostentatious Christianity of the Austen family.

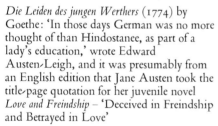

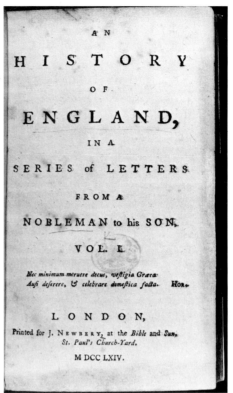

Die Leiden des jungen Werthers (1774) by
Goethe: 'In those days German was no more
thought of than Hindostanee, as part of a
lady's education,' wrote Edward
Austen-Leigh, and it was presumably from
an English edition that Jane Austen took the
title-page quotation for her juvenile novel
Love and Freindship – 'Deceived in Freindship
and Betrayed in Love'

Jane Austen thought it 'proper' to inform
readers of her *History of England* that Anna
Bullen's letter to the King 'was dated on the
6th of May'. This is the only date given in
Oliver Goldsmith's *History of England*, 'very
probably', says Mary Lascelles, 'the
schoolroom history book at Steventon.'

Jane read voraciously, and not only classical authors. The novels of Fielding *Jane Austen's*
and Richardson were as well known to her as the volumes of the *Spectator*, the *Reading*
works of Dr Johnson and Goldsmith's *History of England*. She read Smollett and
Sterne, Sherlock's *Sermons* and Blair's *Rhetoric*, and at an early age was enamoured
of Gilpin on the Picturesque. The poems of Cowper she was devoted to: she let
Marianne Dashwood of *Sense and Sensibility* despise Edward Ferrers's inability to
be 'animated' by them. Moreover, all the family loved novels, and those, with
other books, were read aloud in the evenings. Jane could reach French easily and
a little Italian, could play the piano and sing and dance, and was an excellent
sempstress and embroideress. In short, she (and no doubt Cassandra too) was as ac-
complished as was proper for a girl of her day, and considerably more so than most.

◀ The gateway of the old Abbey at Reading. Mrs Latournelle's Abbey School was in the
Gatehouse

The Parsonage House was emptying of permanent inhabitants, and on their return from school Cassandra and Jane were well accommodated with two rooms on the first floor, a small bedroom and a larger dressing-room or, as we should now call it, sitting-room. Their niece Anna remembered it, furnished with a 'common-looking carpet with its chocolate ground, and painted press with shelves above for books,' – those included Dodsley's Collection of Poems and the five volumes of Samuel Richardson's *Clarissa* – 'and Jane's piano'. There too were kept Cassandra's drawing materials (until fairly recently the ladies of the family thought her drawings as talented as Jane's writings), Jane's desk, a box with a sloping lid; and there was an oval looking-glass between the windows.

The life to which the girls returned was gay and full. Steventon was in the

The Royal Naval Academy at Portsmouth, where Francis and Charles Austen were educated

centre of the Vine Hunt district, and all the boys were keen sportsmen. Francis, at seven, had bought a chestnut pony for £1 11s. 6d. which he called Squirrel; he rode to hounds on Squirrel for two years and then sold him for £2 12s. 6d. Francis was soon to go off to the Royal Naval Academy at Portsmouth which had been founded in 1775, and Charles was to follow him there, but when home on leave, hunting, and still more, shooting, were eagerly sought by them.

When Jane was about eleven a new focus of interest appeared in the Austen family life in the form of cousin Eliza's contributions to their private theatricals. Mr Hancock had brought his wife and daughter home from India in 1764–5. He himself had returned in 1769 and died there in 1775, but Philadelphia and Eliza had remained in Europe, first in England and mostly at Steventon, then, from

Cousin Eliza and Family Theatricals

Madame la Comtesse de Feuillide,
née Eliza Hancock (1761–1813)

Below left, a scene from David
Garrick's comedy *Bon Ton; or, High
Life below Stairs*, which was first
performed at Drury Lane in 1775

Below right, private theatricals in a
grander setting than the barn at
Steventon Rectory, perhaps nearer the
scale of Ecclesford, the seat of the Right
Hon. Lord Ravenshaw in Cornwall,
referred to in Ch. XIII, Vol. I of
Mansfield Park

1780, in Paris where, in 1781, Eliza had married Jean Capotte, Comte de Feuillide. 'He literally adores me', she wrote to her half-cousin Phila Walter.

By all accounts, and by the evidence of her portrait, Eliza was enchanting, and provided a gay, sophisticated leaven in the Austen family life. She came to England again in 1786 for the birth of her son Hastings, and disported herself happily in London and in Tunbridge Wells where she stayed with her mother and Phila Walter. There they went to the theatre and saw two comedies, *Bon Ton* by Garrick and Mrs Cowley's *Which is the Man?* When she went on to Steventon, nothing would suit her but that these plays should be given with some *empressement* in the barn there.

The Austen family were no strangers to family acting. Only three years earlier the barn had seen a performance of Sheridan's *The Rivals*, and of Thomas Francklin's tragedy of *Matilda*, with an epilogue spoken by Thomas Fowle. Plays in the barn at Midsummer and in the dining-room at Christmas, when the pupils went home, became a family custom, but the presence of Eliza lent them a new sparkle. James, just back from a tour in France, wrote the prologues, and Henry and Eliza played the leads.

Phila Walter, though pressed to come and share in the work, stayed at home. Next year, however, she saw Jane on her first visit to Godmersham, and wrote of her half-cousin that she was 'not at all pretty and very prim, unlike a girl of twelve; but it is hasty judgment'.

First Writings

The judgment almost certainly *was* hasty and malapropos. Unlike Cassandra who was devoted to Edward, Jane only seldom visited Godmersham and seems not greatly to have liked it there. By the age of twelve, however, she was already writing profusely. She is said to have helped her brother James with the prologues to the family theatrical performances. Writing rhymed charades was a constant family game, and many of these written over the years, including some of Jane's, have been preserved. (It will be remembered that rhymed charades were a meaningful amusement of Emma's set at Highbury.) More importantly, Jane produced a series of pieces, mostly farcical, mostly fictional, dedicated to members of the family and close friends, and these, by 1793, she had copied into three quarto notebooks which still exist, named by her *Volume the First*, *Volume the Second* and *Volume the Third*.

None of these pieces is discreditable to a girl in her early teens. Some, notably the *History of England* ('N.B. There will be very few dates in this History') are genuinely funny. The farcical novel, *Love and Freindship*, written, as was Jane Austen's other early serious fiction, in the form of letters, has moments of real humour and a substantial appreciation of the absurdities of the popular romantic novels she was parodying. ('It was too pathetic for the feelings of Sophia and myself – We fainted alternately on a sofa!') Indeed, Mr B. C. Southam regards *Love and Freindship* as 'the most amusing and incisive of all eighteenth-century attacks upon sentimental fiction.' He points out that in the readiness of this young girl to joke about 'deformity, injury, death, drunkenness, child-bearing and illegitimacy', as in these short pieces she does, she reveals herself a child of the eighteenth century.

Knowing, as we do, the grandeur of Jane Austen's talent at its maturity, it is hard dispassionately to assess the achievement, as against the promise, of most of those early pieces. There is no evidence that even in her loving and appreciative family they were made much of. After all, the Austens were all talented with the powers of invention that Mrs Austen called 'sprack wit', and many of them could write. Mrs Austen enjoyed writing passable doggerel verse of which some survives. James, as his mother said, possessed the power of elegant composition; at Oxford, between January 1789 and March 1790, he founded and edited a journal called *The Loiterer*, writing, as university editors are apt to do, much of it himself. Henry, when he came up, was a contributor, notably of a paper in the sentimental school of Rousseau; he also wrote verses, as did Charles. As for Cassandra, in addition to her talents with the pencil, she was, according to Jane, 'the finest comic writer

An illustration to *La Nouvelle Héloïse* by
J. J. Rousseau, characteristic of the
sentimental school which tickled Henry
Austen's pen at Oxford

of the age' – but of this we have no firsthand evidence. Nor do we know that Francis wrote, but he was immensely deft with his hands, fond of making toys for the children of the family, such as a little milkchurn which he turned for one of Edward's daughters. In any case, when Jane was in her teens, there were more interesting things to think of in the Austen household than the possibility that one of its members might become a professional novelist.

Of those, one of the most important was the social life of the neighbourhood *Social Life* and the part the Austen girls might play in it. They were fortunate in the many convivial families near by (some of whom are still there), the Jervoises of Herriard, the Terrys, and, rather more socially elevated, the Boltons and the Portsmouths. Steventon Manor, with an absentee landlord, was rented to a friendly family, the Digwoods, and Deane House was occupied by the ball-giving Harwoods. Closer friends were the Bigg-Wither family at Manydown House near Basingstoke. (On receiving an inheritance, the father and son took the name of Bigg-Wither; the daughters, among them the Austen girls' special friends, Elizabeth, Catherine and Alethea, retained the simple Bigg.) Cassandra and Jane were used to spend the night at Manydown House when they went to the balls held in the assembly rooms of the Angel Inn at Basingstoke, since even on moonlit nights, when entertainments most conveniently took place, the drive back from Basingstoke to Steventon would have been over-long.

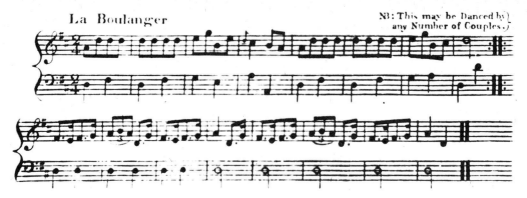

La Boulanger

NB: This may be Danced by any Number of Couples.

The music of the Boulanger. 'We dined at Goodnestone & in the Evening danced two Country Dances and the Boulangeries.' (*Letter* from JA to Cassandra, 5 September 1796)

Left, a mid-nineteenth-century trade card of the Angel Inn, Basingstoke, in whose Assembly Rooms Jane Austen often went to balls

Left below, Manydown near Basingstoke, home of the Bigg-Wither family, where the Austen girls often stayed

Below, gentlefolk in the English countryside

The Lloyds   But the most important of the close friends were the occupants of the houses of the two livings bought by Uncle Francis Austen. That of Deane, George Austen's own subsidiary living, was occupied by a family called Lloyd. The father, the Rev. Nowys Lloyd, had died in 1789, leaving Mrs Lloyd with three daughters. The second, Eliza, had married her first cousin, Fulwar Craven Fowle, Vicar of Kintbury in Wiltshire; the eldest and youngest, Martha and Mary, were at home.

Mrs Lloyd's mother was an extraordinary and melodramatic figure. An extremely beautiful woman, she was justly known by her descendants as the cruel Mrs Craven, for she treated her daughters abominably, beating them, starving them, and locking them up, until at last in desperation they ran away from home and, fortunately, made safe marriages. It was probably the cruel Mrs Craven whom Jane Austen had in mind when she was later to create her Lady Susan.

When the Austens had come to Steventon in 1764, the Rectory at Ashe had been occupied by Dr Russell, the grandfather of the writer Mary Russell Mitford. In 1783 he had died and the new incumbent, the Rev. Isaac Lefroy, a former Fellow of All Souls, and his wife, Anne, often referred to as Madam Lefroy, were the greatest of assets to the neighbourhood. Mrs Lefroy seems to have been a charming woman and, in particular, a close and loving friend to Jane Austen. Moreover, by opening the folding doors between their dining-room and morning-room, the Lefroys were able to give dances at which several couples could stand up.

Anne Lefroy   We have quite a few descriptions of Jane Austen at about the period when she could be considered as 'coming out'. Mrs Lefroy's brother, the writer Sir Egerton Brydges, who had rented the parsonage house at Deane before the Lloyds moved there, wrote later that 'she was fair and handsome, slight and elegant, but with cheeks a little too full.' Eliza de Feuillide in 1791 several times wrote generously of her cousins. Cassandra and Jane were 'very much grown (the latter is now taller than myself) and greatly improved in manners as in person.' She had heard that they were 'perfect Beauties, and of course gain hearts of dozens', and again, of Cassandra, 'I hear her sister and herself are two of the prettiest girls in England.' More prosaically, Henry Austen, in his biographical notice to the posthumous edition of *Northanger Abbey* and *Persuasion*, wrote,

> Of personal attractions she possessed a considerable share. Her stature was that of true elegance. It could not have been increased without exceeding the middle height. Her carriage and deportment were quiet, yet graceful. Her features were separately good. Their assemblage produced an unrivalled expression of that cheerfulness, sensibility, and benevolence, which were her real characteristics. Her complexion was of the finest texture. It might with truth be said, that her eloquent blood spoke through her modest cheek.

34

Mary Russell (Mrs Mitford) at the age of three. Her grandfather, Dr Russell,
had preceded the Rev. Isaac Lefroy as Rector of Ashe

The Rev. Isaac Lefroy, Rector of Ashe

Sir Egerton Brydges, Madam Lefroy's brother

Overton, between Basingstoke and Steventon: James Austen's first curacy

This somewhat pompous tribute was, it should be remembered, written after Jane Austen's death, and, no doubt, was rather an impression of her in her middle years than in her youth. Of the earlier period, and while Jane Austen was still alive, Mary Russell Mitford recalled her mother as saying that Jane Austen had been 'the prettiest, silliest, most affected, husband-hunting butterfly' that she ever remembered. Those who will allow Jane Austen nothing but virtues have denied the possibility of this portrait's truth by pointing out that the Russells had left Ashe in 1783 when Jane was only eight. But they had moved only to the town of Alresford, not far away, and it is likely that gossip of Steventon and its neighbour-hood would still have interested them; indeed, there may still have been social meetings. In any case, the portrait is not an unattractive one.

But before Jane Austen herself could have been seriously husband-hunting, the older members of her family were already getting married and, alas, widowed.

Edward Austen (1768–1852). He changed his surname to Knight in 1812

Elizabeth Austen *née* Bridges (1773–1808), wife of Edward Austen

The first marriage, in 1791, was that of Edward to the beautiful Elizabeth Bridges, daughter of Sir Brook Bridges, a neighbour in Kent. The young couple settled at a small house, Rowlings, near Godmersham, and in 1793 Fanny Catherine, the first of what was to be a family of eleven children, was born.

James, after a period as Fellow of his College, had left Oxford, and in 1792 had a curacy at Overton, near Steventon. (Steventon letters were postmarked at Overton.) In this year he married Anne Mathew, daughter of General Mathew, the tenant of nearby Laverstoke House. Anne was five years older than her husband, but 'a very pretty woman', said kind Eliza. The young couple were comfortably off; James kept a pack of harriers, and Mrs James a carriage. General Mathew allowed his daughter £100 a year, and James had £200 a year of his own, as well as the incumbency of Deane, from which the Lloyds now removed, going to a house at Ibthrop, near Hurstbourne Tarrant, not far away. On their going, Jane Austen made Mary Lloyd a miniscule hussif of gingham containing miniature needles and fine thread, and, in its tiny pocket, a poem written in a tiny hand, as with a crow⁄quill: 'This little bag, I hope, will prove,/To be not vainly made;/For should you thread and needles want,/It will afford you aid./And as we are about to part,/ 'Twill serve another end:/For when you look upon this bag,/'Twill recollect your friend.'

The uniform that Henry Austen would have worn as an officer in the Oxford Militia

Celebration of Bastille Day in Paris, 1792; two years later the Comte de Feuillide was to die on the guillotine

Jane Anne Elizabeth Austen, James's daughter, was born the following year. Two years later, in 1795, her mother died, and little Anna was sent for the time being to Steventon, to be brought up by her grandparents and her aunts.

Eliza, too, had known misfortune. In 1791 her mother, Mrs Hancock, had died, and in 1794 her husband, the Comte de Feuillide, having returned to France to try to save his estates, had died on the guillotine, brought to the scaffold through an apparently harmless attempt to help a friend. Thereafter Eliza, with her delicate little son Hastings, was much at Steventon.

As to the other Austen boys, Henry, after University, had joined the Oxford-shire Militia, while Francis and Charles were at the start of what were to be long and distinguished careers in the Navy. Francis, by 1792 a Lieutenant, had been on a cruise to the East Indies, and Charles, as a Midshipman, went to the Mediterranean; in 1796 his ship the *Unicorn*, under Captain Thomas Williams who was now married to Cousin Jane Cooper, captured two French ships in a spirited and publicized action.

The English frigate *Unicorn* in action against the French frigate *La Tribune* on 8 June 1796

'Your best friend upon such an occasion', said Miss Bertram calmly, 'would be Mr Repton, I imagine' (*Mansfield Park*, Ch. VI, Vol. I), but Miss Bertram's fiancé, Mr Rushworth, protested

Jane Austen's Letters   The second part of the 1790s were full and interesting years for Jane Austen, both as regards her personal and family life and her life as a writer. Our under-standing of the former is enormously enhanced by her letters (or perhaps it would be better to say her surviving letters), which start in January 1796.

Almost all are written to Cassandra, and they are addressed to Miss Austen, the correct mode of address for the eldest unmarried daughter of a family; Cas-sandra's replies to Jane would have been addressed to Miss Jane Austen, the correct mode of address for any but the eldest daughter. Jane Austen, like most people of her class and time, was punctilious in observing such conventions as these. In *Mansfield Park*, for example, Tom Bertram, the elder son, is Mr Bertram, and much is made of the fact that were he to die, his younger brother, Mr Edmund Bertram, would become Mr Bertram in his stead. The elder sister Maria is until her marriage always spoken of respectfully as Miss Bertram and her younger sister as Miss Julia Bertram. This convention, though eroded, still holds good, and Miss Jane Austen would have had small patience with those who now speak of her, albeit with affectionate reverence, as Miss Austen.

Undoubtedly Jane Austen's letters add a new dimension to her personality, but opinions differ as to the impression we receive from them. Certainly they are malicious, and those admirers who will allow Jane Austen nothing short of perfection are hard put to it to soften such a notorious comment as: 'Mrs. Hall, of

Cassandra Elizabeth Austen
(1773–1845)

that Mr Repton's terms were five guineas a day. Had he been engaged, he would no doubt have improved the grounds of Sotherton Court in some such manner as this

Sherbourne, was brought to bed yesterday of a dead child, some weeks before she expected, owing to a fright. I suppose she happened unawares to look at her husband', or of neighbours, the Misses Debary, 'I was as civil to them as their bad breath would allow me.' On the other hand one must remember that the early letters, from 1796 to 1801, were written almost entirely to her sister Cassandra, with whom her relationship was closer than with any other human being. And reading through the letters, through the asperities, through the accounts of frivolities and shopping, and all shot through by enchanting wit, we gain the impression of a distinct *persona* established in the relationship between the sisters, a *persona* detached, mocking, above being 'put-upon' or taken in, which was not necessarily the *persona* presented by Miss Jane Austen to the rest of the world.

There is another important respect in which, it must be remembered, the letters offer only a partial picture of Jane Austen's life, and this in addition to Cassandra's later excisions and suppressions. The letters were written only when the sisters were separated, and so we lack Jane's comments on any important event that took place when they were together. But fortunately for us they were often apart, since paying prolonged visits was an important part of the Austen family life. We hear of journeys, made or projected, to the Lloyds at Ibthrop, to Edward and his growing family in Kent, to Adlestrop (this would be to stay with the Leigh relations), and to Great Bookham, the home of Jane's godfather, the Rev. Samuel Cooke.

James Leigh Perrot
(17..–1817), Mrs Geroge
Austen's brother

There were also visits to Bath, no longer, as some fifty years earlier, a smart resort of high life. That palm was passing to Brighton where Jane Austen sent naughty Lydia Bennet but where, she wrote, she did not wish to go herself. Bath at the end of the eighteenth century had become a solid respectable town, the home of many a retired clergyman, and visited as a resort rather for health than for gaiety, a suitable second home for the ultra-respectable Elliots of *Persuasion*, an exciting first venture into the world for a young, unsophisticated Catherine Morland, but unlikely to tempt, say, a Henry or Mary Crawford except when they were dutifully accompanying an elderly relation there. Jane Austen and her mother went to Bath in 1799 on a luxurious holiday with Edward and his wife and children, and her letters from Bath to Cassandra, full of gaieties and frivolities, are charming. Edward, however, had gone there not for gaiety but for health. He seems, at times,

Axford and Paragon Buildings, Bath

to have bid fair to be as great a hypochondriac as his mother, of whom, in 1798, Jane wrote to Cassandra, 'My mother continues hearty, her appetite & nights are very good, but her Bowels are still not entirely settled, & she sometimes complains of an Asthma, a Dropsy, Water in her Chest & a Liver Disorder.'

We do not gain the impression of there being much deep affection or close understanding between Jane Austen and her mother, though never of a failure of duty.

There were almost certainly other visits to Bath – we hear of invitations being given – for at Paragon Buildings, Bath, there lived for half the year Mrs Austen's wealthy brother, James Leigh Perrot and his wife. The Leigh Perrots, whose other home was Scarlets, in Berkshire, were childless, and it was confidently expected that James Austen would be their heir. In 1799, they were involved in a strange scandal.

Jane, wife of James Leigh Perrot (1744–1836)

Pump of the King's Bath at Bath

ACCOUNT *of the* TRIAL *of Mrs.* LEIGH PERROT, *charged with stealing a card of lace in the shop of Elizabeth Gregory, haberdasher and milliner, at Bath, which came on, on Saturday morning the 29th of March,* 1800, *at the Somerset assizes, held at Taunton, before Mr. Justice Lawrence.*

(Embellished with an elegant Portrait of Mrs. Leigh Perrot.)

ABOUT half past seven o'clock, the prisoner, attended by a number of ladies, walked from their lodgings at the London inn, in two or three different parties, to the Assize-hall, about a quarter of a mile, where they waited, in the anti-room to the grand-jury-room, till the judge came, about eight o'clock. She then went into the prisoner's pen, accompanied by her husband, Mrs. Winstone, and

The indictment consisted of four counts, varying the owner of the property charged to have been stolen. Her counsel requested she might be allowed a chair, which was granted.

The counsel for the prosecution were Mr. Gibbs and Mr. Burrough; for the prisoner Mr. Bond, Mr. Dallas, Mr. Jekyll, and Mr. Pell.

The prosecution having been opened by Mr. Burrough—

Mr. Gibbs then addressed the jury. In his speech he confined himself to stating the situation of the parties, of the prosecutor's shop, and the evidence that he was about to adduce in support of the prosecution, and then proceeded to call his witnesses in the following order:

Elizabeth Gregory deposed, that in August last she kept a haberdasher's shop in Bath-street, in the

An account of Mrs Leigh Perrot's trial in *The Lady's Magazine*, April 1800

Mrs Leigh Perrot was taken up at Bath on a charge of petty theft, accused of stealing a small quantity of lace from a shop. Though the charge was a trumped-up one, apparently with the intention of blackmail (as was quickly shown at the trial the following year), Mrs Leigh Perrot, accompanied by her husband, spent eight months in Ilchester jail, with the possibility of transportation were she convicted. Cassandra and Jane both offered to come and stay with her in prison but fortunately, no doubt, for their health, the offer was refused.

First Love-Affair

In addition to the pleasures of dancing and visiting and shopping, the second half of the '90s were also, and not surprisingly, marked by affairs of the heart for both Jane and Cassandra. When the letters begin, Jane is in the middle of the first love-affair that we know about (there is a hint of an earlier, perhaps childish infatuation in Kent). It is with Tom Lefroy, a handsome young Irish cousin of the Lefroys of Ashe.

This could come to nothing and everyone knew it. Tom Lefroy was ambitious. He had no money, Jane Austen had no money, and Tom Lefroy must acquire money through marriage. Notwithstanding this, the young couple seem to have made something of an exhibition of themselves in the neighbourhood, and Jane,

Thomas Langlois Lefroy (1776–1869). 'He is a very gentlemanlike, good-looking, pleasant young man, I assure you.' (*Letter* from JA to Cassandra, 9 January 1796)

kindly cautioned by both Mrs Lefroy and Cassandra, responded with the defiant petulance usual in such cases:

> You scold me so much in the nice long letter which I have this moment received from you, that I am almost afraid to tell you how my Irish friend and I behaved. Imagine to yourself everything most profligate and shocking in the way of dancing and sitting down together. I *can* expose myself, however, only *once more*, because he leaves the country soon after next Friday. . . .

Tom Lefroy left. He made a suitable marriage and eventually became Lord Chief Justice of Ireland. In his old age, his nephew asked him about the affair with Jane Austen. 'He did not state in what her fascination consisted, but he said in so many words that he was in love with her, although he qualified his confession by saying that it was a boyish love.'

There is no reason to suppose that on Jane Austen's side, either, it was more than a girlish love, or that her heart was deeply or lastingly touched. Her next suitor seems not to have touched her heart at all.

He was a Mr Samuel Blackall, a Fellow of Emmanuel College, Cambridge, who met Jane Austen when he was staying with the Lefroys in 1798. Afterwards he wrote to Mrs Lefroy saying that he would like to improve his acquaintance with the Austen family – 'with a hope of creating to myself a nearer interest. But at present I cannot indulge any expectation of it.' Jane commented, 'This is rational enough; there is less love and more sense in it than sometimes appeared before, and I am very well satisfied. It will all go on exceedingly well, and decline away in a very reasonable manner.' And so, apparently, it did, for we do not hear of Mr Blackall again until 1813 when he married a Miss Susanna Lewis, and Jane Austen wrote to her brother Francis, 'I would wish Miss Lewis to be of a silent turn & rather ignorant, but naturally intelligent & wishing to learn; – fond of cold veal pies, green tea in the afternoon, & a green window blind at night.'

Cassandra's love affair was serious and tragic. In 1795 she became engaged to that Thomas Fowle who had been a pupil at Steventon Rectory, the brother of the Vicar of Kintbury who had married Eliza Lloyd. Again there was no money, but in this case neither Thomas nor Cassandra, nor, indeed, their respective families minded it. A modicum, however, there must be, and all that was in prospect from Thomas's patron, Lord Craven, was the promise of the living of Ryton in Shropshire, with no more income than might suffice for a bachelor. On this, which lay a couple of years ahead, they decided to marry, but for the meantime Lord Craven offered Thomas the post of Chaplain to his regiment which was going out to the West Indies. After much anxious discussion the offer was accepted, for the prospect it offered of saving money against the marriage. The almost inevitable happed. Thomas sailed in 1796 and in February 1797 died at Santo Domingo of yellow fever. Lord Craven said afterwards that had he known that Thomas Fowle was engaged, he would never have let him go.

Eliza wrote, 'Jane says that her sister behaves with a degree of resolution and propriety, which no common mind could evince in so trying a situation.' 'I believe,' wrote Miss Mary Lascelles of Jane Austen and this sad episode, 'that if she ever allows the substance of actual experience, imperfectly transmuted, to enter a novel it is in her defence of Elinor Dashwood and her explicit protest, there, that fortitude has nothing to do with insensibility.'

We do not hear that Cassandra ever considered marriage again, but there were, during those years, marriages in the Austen family. James had been looking for a second wife. He had considered his pretty cousin Eliza, who is said to have refused him on grounds that recall Mary Crawford, that she did not want to marry a clergyman. In the event, in 1797, James married pock-marked Mary Lloyd, and Henry, by now a Captain in the Oxfordshire Militia, after a flirtation with a Miss Pearson, married Eliza.

At the latter marriage Mrs Austen was displeased. Though Mr Austen was

The Rev. Samuel Blackall, who had hoped to improve his acquaintance with Jane Austen in 1798, was a Fellow of Emmanuel College, Cambridge, like the gentlemen depicted here at left

Santo Domingo in the West Indies, where Cassandra Austen's fiancé, Thomas Fowle, died of yellow fever in February, 1797

fond of Eliza, his wife never had a good word to say for her and in any case had hoped that Henry would marry Martha Lloyd – who did eventually become her daughter-in-law, but much later and by marriage to another son. Mrs Austen's letter to Mary on the engagement was surely written as much against Eliza as to Mary – 'you, my dear Mary, are the person I should have chosen for James's wife, Anna's mother and my daughter.'

Mary and James had two children, James Edward, Jane Austen's future biographer, born in 1798, and a daughter Caroline Mary Craven, born in 1805. Eliza and Henry had no children; Eliza's son Hastings, by her first marriage, died of epilepsy in 1801. But the handsome, gay, sophisticated pair were well enough suited, even though Eliza was ten years the older. Henry left the militia, and with two other officers started a firm of Army bankers, Austen, Maude, and Tilson, with offices in London where he and Eliza thereafter lived – fortunately for us, since Jane Austen often visited them there, and letters from their various homes, in Upper Berkeley Street, in Michael's Place, Brompton, and in Sloane Street, were written to Cassandra.

The last important family event of those years concerned Edward Austen. Thomas Knight, his adoptive father, had died in 1794. In 1798 Mrs Knight, his widow, generously made over Godmersham Park to Edward, moving to a small house, White Friars near Canterbury, and retaining only £2,000 a year for herself. Thereafter visits by Jane or, more often, Cassandra to Edward and Elizabeth were made to a handsome mansion in the classical style where life was lived with a luxury that contrasted strongly with the simplicity of the Hampshire Austens. Jane had perhaps forgotten the difference money can make when she contrasted the lyings-in of her two sisters-in-law:

> Mary does not manage matters in such a way as to make me want to lay in myself. She is not tidy enough in her appearance; she has no dressing-gown to sit up in; her curtains are all too thin, and things are not in that comfort and style about her which are necessary to make such a situation an enviable one. Elizabeth was really a pretty object with her nice clean cap put on so tidily and her dress so uniformly white and orderly.

With writings and dancings and affairs of the heart one might have thought those years full enough. But they were also the first of the two great creative periods of Jane Austen's life.

'Elinor and Marianne'

The copying of the notebooks had been completed in 1793. During 1795 she was writing a novel in letters called *Elinor and Marianne*, the first version of the story that was eventually to become *Sense and Sensibility*. (She was not the only story-maker in the dressing-room; her little niece Anna, constantly told stories by Aunt Jane,

Portman Square, London; behind the lamp-post can be seen Upper Berkeley Street where Henry and Eliza Austen were living in 1801

began, in her turn, to dictate stories to be written down, and a drama founded on *Sir Charles Grandison*, dictated by Anna at the age of seven, still exists in Jane's handwriting.) *Elinor and Marianne* was sufficiently finished to be read to the family by 1796, and in October of this year Jane Austen began a new novel, which she then called *First Impressions*. This was the first version of *Pride and Prejudice*.

'*First Impressions*'

There are a couple of references to *First Impressions* in the early letters. 'I do not wonder at your wanting to read "First Impressions" again, so seldom as you have gone through it, and that so long ago. I am much obliged to you for meaning to leave my old petticoat behind you', Jane wrote to Cassandra in January 1799, and later in the same year she wrote jokingly that Martha was not to read *First Impressions* again: 'She is very cunning, but I saw through her design; she means to publish it from memory, and one more perusal must enable her to do it.'

49

We also have some account of the early days of *First Impressions* from Anna, now old enough to take notice. While playing in the dressing-room, she would hear Cassandra's bursts of laughter as Jane read the book aloud to her. Anna got to know the story and the people in it, and began to talk of it downstairs, until the sisters warned her that she must keep it a secret.

'Susan' Probably in 1798 Jane Austen began another book called *Susan*, which was eventually to become *Northanger Abbey*. All the Austen family were great readers, and great readers aloud. New books were constantly procured, whether from Mrs Martin's local subscription library or by purchase; the name of Miss J. Austen is on the subscription list for Fanny Burney's *Camilla*, published in 1796. The Austen family had none of the common contempt for novels. When Mrs Martin opened her subscription library in 1798, she offered as an inducement to sub-scribers the information that she would have not only novels but every kind of literature. This Jane Austen rejected with contempt: 'She might have spared this pretension to *our* family, who are great Novel-readers & not ashamed of being so' – a passage to set beside her famous defence of the novel in *Northanger Abbey*. So Jane Austen would not have missed the publication, in 1794, of Mrs Radcliffe's melodramatic 'Gothick' novel, *The Mysteries of Udolpho*, and to parody it in her *Susan* must have been irresistible.

'Lady Susan' Another book that almost certainly belongs to this period is her epistolatory novel *Lady Susan*, the story of the cruel fashionable mother and her ill-treated

Madame d'Arblay (Fanny Burney). She
was acquainted with the Cookes of
Great Bookham, and it is possible that
Jane Austen met her in Surrey

An illustration from the 1803 edition of
The Mysteries of Udolpho by
Ann Radcliffe

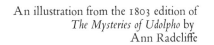

The Circulating Library in
Milsom Street, Bath

daughter. The surviving manuscript is on paper watermarked 1805, but this is a fair copy. For all the story's merits, it undoubtedly reveals itself an early work when compared with the capable maturity of the great novels.

The similarity of the titles *Susan* and *Lady Susan* might suggest that the latter work had originally a different name, but this is not necessarily so. For all her care and delight in place names, to the names of people Jane Austen was surprisingly insensitive. There were, after all, very few Christian names among her own near relations and those she used over and over again. Not only did she use her own name, Jane, which is distinctly unusual – Jane Bennet, Jane Fairfax; she also used her sisters-in-law's names apparently indiscriminately for quite different types of person – 'nice' Elizabeth Bennet and 'nasty' Elizabeth Elliot, naughty charming Mary Crawford and dull petulant Mary Musgrove.

Only one attempt at publication seems to have been made during those years. By 1797 *First Impressions* had apparently been read to the family, for on 1 November of that year Jane Austen's father wrote to the publisher Cadell that he had in his possession 'a manuscript novel, comprising 3 vols., about the length of Miss Burney's Evelina.' Would the publisher care to see it with a view to publication, perhaps at the author's expense? The publisher would not.

This period of literary fecundity closed with a great change that came over the Austen family life. In November 1800, Cassandra was at Godmersham and Jane at Ibthrop visiting the Lloyds. On 30 November Jane returned home bringing Martha Lloyd with her. As they entered the house Mrs Austen greeted them with *From Steventon* 'Well girls! It is all settled. We have decided to leave Steventon and go to Bath', *to Bath* and on hearing this Jane fainted.

The decision must have been a sudden one. Only that year, indeed only that very month, improvements were being planned for the Steventon garden. But George Austen was nearly seventy, and probably felt himself ripe for retirement, the more so since he had in James a son ready to take over what had virtually become a family living. Jane, however, stoutly regarded herself as a 'Hampshire-born Austen' and seems to have felt somewhat like her own Anne Elliot who 'persisted in a very determined, though silent, disinclination for Bath.' However, Jane made a gallant attempt to make the best of it and entered, though with obvious boredom and uninterest, into what were to prove lengthy discussions as to what were to be done with books and furniture, what servants should be employed, and where in Bath they were to settle.

In the event books and furniture were left behind or sold and in 1801 Mr and Mrs Austen with their two daughters removed to Bath, at first staying in the Paragon with the Leigh Perrots, eventually, after much house-hunting, settling at 4 Sydney Place, with the advantage of the Sydney Gardens before the house – 'we might go into the Labyrinth every day,' Jane wrote with forced cheerfulness to

Cassandra. One other benefit she had hopefully looked forward to from the move: 'the prospect of spending future summers by the Sea or in Wales is very delightful.' Though the Austens never, as far as we know, went to Wales, they did go to the sea. But for Jane, this expected pleasure turned to dust and ashes.

We know the story only imperfectly as it was accidentally revealed by Cassandra, long after Jane's death, at the sight of a young man who reminded her of this lost lover. As told by Mrs Bellas, Anna's daughter, this is what happened:

> In the summer of 1801, the father, mother and daughters made a tour in Devonshire. I believe it was at the last named place [probably Sidmouth but possibly Teignmouth] that they made acquaintance with a young clergyman then visiting his brother, who was one of the doctors of the town. He and Jane fell in love with each other, and when the Austens left he asked to be allowed to join them again further on in their tour, and the permission was given. But instead of his arriving as expected, they received a letter announcing his death. In Aunt Cassandra's memory he lived as one of the most charming persons she had ever known, worthy even in her eyes of Aunt Jane.

Morning dress, 1801 (right). 'Bonnets of cambric muslin on the plan of Lady Bridges' are a great deal worn, and some of them are very pretty.' (*Letter* from JA to Cassandra, 5 May 1801)

Sydney Gardens, Bath. 'It would be very pleasant to be near Sydney Gardens.' (*Letter* from JA to Cassandra, 21 January 1801)

Of contemporary evidence of the story we have none. But between May 1801 and September 1804, no letters of Jane Austen's survive.

Offer of Marriage

One further attempt, however, was to be made on her heart. In November 1802, Cassandra and Jane were staying with the Bigg-Withers at Manydown. On the morning of 3 December they appeared at the Steventon Rectory in great agitation, insisting without explanation and with unusual lack of consideration that James should drive them back to Bath the next day, even though this meant that he would have to find a substitute to preach for him that Sunday. Gradually it emerged that Harris Bigg-Wither, the 21-year-old son of the house, had proposed to Jane the night before and had been accepted by her. Despite the discrepancy in age (Jane was then 27), it was obviously an excellent match, a Hampshire match into a well-endowed family of old friends. But in the morning Jane discovered that she could not go through with it. Her niece Caroline said long afterwards, 'To be sure she should not have said "Yes" overnight, but I have always respected her for cancelling that "yes" the next morning.' It is pleasant to record that this episode did not mar the friendship between the Austen and Bigg sisters, and later Cassandra, at least, is to be found staying at Manydown again.

The years at Bath, then, were unhappy and dull. There was the mitigation of family visits, and, for what they were worth, more 'tours' to the seaside, to Teignmouth and to Dawlish, and, in 1803 and 1804, significantly in relation to its

View of Dawlish

The Bathing Place at Ramsgate by Benjamin West

importance in *Persuasion*, to Lyme. Jane also went to Ramsgate to visit her brother Francis, who was engaged there in organizing the 'Sea Fencibles' against the expected invasion from France, and to visit too her future sister-in-law, Mary Gibson, whom Frank had met there and whom he married in 1806. A new sorrow struck Jane Austen in 1804 with the death of her especial friend, Mrs Lefroy of Ashe, by a fall from a horse – the second death in the circle from a road accident, for Cousin Jane Williams *née* Cooper, driving herself in a one-horse chaise in 1798, had collided with a dray-horse, and was thrown out and picked up dead. Mrs Lefroy's death was a sore blow to Jane, and on it she wrote her only known serious poem, a poem of deep feeling if small poetic merit.

'The Watsons' Started and Abandoned

From the letters written before the break of May 1801, we gain a miserable impression of the social life of Bath as it was for the Austen girls: some uninspiring visits to the Assembly Rooms, a few walks in the neighbourhood, some visiting with people of no great interest. Only one original work was started, the novel *The Watsons* (the paper of the manuscript is watermarked 1803), and this was abandoned in 1805 after only some 17,500 words had been written. Edward Austen-Leigh, in his Memoir, suggested that this was because Jane Austen realized 'the evil of having placed her heroine too low, in such a situation of poverty and obscurity as, though not necessarily connected with vulgarity, has a sad tendency to degenerate into it.' We recall the Prices, Jane Fairfax, Mrs Smith, and must think Edward Austen-Leigh's explanation rather a mid-Victorian gloss than the most likely reason. Jane Austen's books were always talked over in

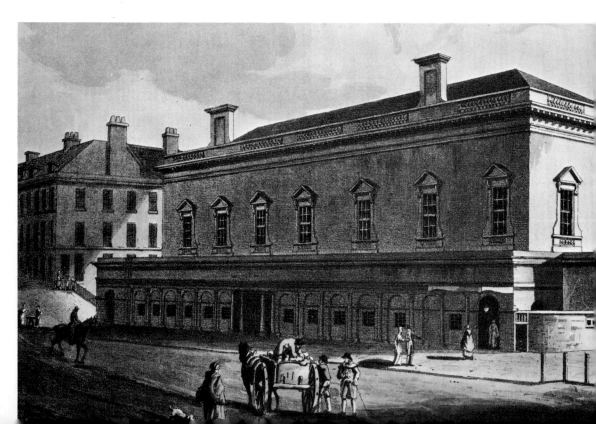

the family, and from them we learn that Emma Watson was to refuse a peer and marry a clergyman. The Inn in the town of D—— was, we are told, the Red Lion at Dorking, which Jane Austen probably knew from visits to the Cookes at Great Bookham, not far away.

One literary possibility did seem to open out during this time when, in 1803, the manuscript of *Susan* was sold to the publisher Crosby for £10 by a Mr Seymour, almost certainly Henry's man of business. The story was sold for immediate publication, and in *Flowers of Literature* for 1801–2 (actually published in 1803) Crosby's advertisement included '"Susan", a Novel in 2 Volumes'. But this venture too failed. For whatever reason *Susan* was never brought out by Crosby.

First Manuscript Sold

The summer holidays, however, were giving some pleasure again, and in 1804 the Austens were at Lyme with Henry and Eliza who eventually moved on to Weymouth, taking Cassandra with them. The first letter of Jane's that Cassandra preserved after the spring of 1801 is dated from Lyme in 1804, and from it we learn that Jane was fond of bathing, believed she had stayed in the water so long as to tire herself, had danced at the local Assembly, and had visited a Mrs Armstrong who 'sat darning a pair of stockings the whole of my visit. But I do not mention this at home, lest a warning should act as an example.' Of course she walked on the Cobb, Lyme's famous stone jetty; and many years later, when Tennyson visited Lyme, he refused all refreshment on his arrival, saying, 'Now take me to the Cobb and show me the steps from which Louisa Musgrove fell.'

The New Assembly Rooms at Bath, 1806

57

View of Dorking, Surrey

View from Polsden near Bookham, Surrey

View of Lyme Regis

In 1804 the Austens left Sydney Place for a house in Green Park Buildings, nearer to the Pump Room for Mr Austen who could now walk only with a stick.

On 19 January 1805, he felt unwell. Next day he got up and breakfasted with the family, but soon afterwards he had a feverish attack and sank into a stupor. He died at 10.20 a.m. on 21 January, and was buried at Walcot Church, Bath, where he had been married. Jane Austen wrote two letters to her brother Frank announcing this sad event; she had feared the first might miss him. No one, reading these letters, can doubt the essential piety of her Christianity, or can be surprised that among her writings are to be found some prayers composed by herself.

Until Mr Austen's death, his family had been if not prosperous at least comfortably off, able to maintain an establishment served by a man and two maids. Now their income was only £210 a year, and this included the interest of £1,000 left to Cassandra by Thomas Fowle.

The Pump Room, Bath

View of Clifton Rocks

The sons came to the rescue. Edward, as became the richest, gave £100 a year, and James, Henry and Frank £50 each (Charles was still away in the West Indies), thus providing Mrs Austen and her daughters with £460 a year. For the time being they left Green Park Buildings for 25 Gay Street, a smaller house needing only one maid, though in a more fashionable part of Bath. There they were joined by Martha Lloyd. Her mother had died at Ibthrop in April, and thereafter she was to make her home with the Austens, a great help to Cassandra and Jane who would be able to make prolonged visits without fear of leaving Mrs Austen alone.

The Austens made one more move in Bath. In April 1806 they were in Trim *Clifton* Street and then, in June, went to Clifton, leaving Bath for ever. In 1808 Jane wrote

61

The cloakroom at an Assembly Rooms Ball: 'Your silence on the subject of our Ball, makes me suppose your curiosity too great for words. We were very well entertained, and could have staid longer but for the arrival of my List shoes to convey me home, and I did not like to keep them waiting in the cold.' (*Letter* from JA to Cassandra, 24 January 1809, after a ball at the Southampton Assembly Rooms)

to Cassandra, 'It will be two years tomorrow since we left Bath for Clifton, with what happy feelings of Escape!' From Clifton they went on to the Rev. Thomas Leigh at Adlestrop, and while they were there Lord Leigh, the owner of Stoneleigh Abbey, died. The Rev. Thomas Leigh inherited, but by a curious will, capable of misinterpretation: Mr Leigh Perrot, for instance, had a possible claim, which he relinquished for £24,000 down and £2,000 a year. Thomas Leigh was advised to take possession immediately, and so in August he removed to Stoneleigh, and Mrs Austen and her daughters went with him, thus giving Cassandra and Jane some taste of what it was like to live on a really grand scale.

Southampton Meanwhile, plans for the future were being made. Frank Austen had married Mary Gibson on 24 July, and it was settled that he and his wife, his mother and his sisters should all set up house together in Southampton which was, for him, conveniently near to Portsmouth. So in the autumn, pending the suitable house, they all moved into lodgings there.

62

The house was found in Castle Square, a pleasant if curious situation, for in the middle of the square the landlord, Lord Lansdowne, had built a miniature castle from which tenants could watch the Marchioness emerging in a light phaeton drawn by six and sometimes eight ponies in graduated shades of brown. The Austens took to homemaking with enthusiasm. Frank, always clever with his hands, was to be found knotting fringe for curtains, and Jane was planning the garden – 'I could not do without a Syringa, for the sake of Cowper's Line. – We talk also of a Laburnam.' Mr Austen had been used to read Cowper to the family, and the lines she had in mind were from the *Winter Walk*, where the poet thinks of spring and:

> '. . . *Laburnum, rich*
> *In streaming gold; syringa, iv'ry pure.'*

This silhouette was found in 1944, pasted in a volume of the second edition of *Mansfield Park*, with the legend 'L'aimable Jane' in an unknown handwriting. 'Who', writes Dr Chapman, 'would insert in a copy of *Mansfield Park*, a portrait of any other Jane than its author?'

The only fly in the immediate ointment was a visit from James who seems, like his wife, to have become rather tiresome. 'Mary begins to fancy,' Jane was to write in 1808, 'because she had received no message on the subject, that Anna does not mean to answer her Letter; but it must be for the pleasure of fancying it'; and in 1807, the family was glad to see James go again: 'his Chat seems all forced, his Opinions on too many points too much copied from his Wife's, & his time here is spent I think in walking about the House & banging the doors, or ringing the bell for a glass of water.' The James Austens seem, too, to have been over-careful with money, though they were comfortably off. The first Mrs James Austen's allowance from her father of £100 a year had been continued for Anna, and in 1808 Mr Leigh Perrot allowed James £100 a year as a token of his admiration for James's refusal of Lord Craven's offer of the living of Hampstead Marshall on the death of old Mr Fowle. The intention was that James should keep it warm for a few years till a younger Fowle could take over, but he felt scruples on the grounds of pluralism and declined it. Mr Leigh Perrot's gift, however, brought his income up to £1,100 a year, with his curate paid.

Now that they were settled, the Austen girls could start visiting again. In the spring of 1808 Jane was with Henry and Eliza at 16 St Michael's Place, Brompton (now the site of Egerton Mansions), and from there she went on to pay one of her rare visits to Godmersham, where she was delighted with Edward and Elizabeth's eldest child, Fanny. In the autumn when she was back at Southampton and Cassandra, in her turn, at Godmersham, Jane wrote, 'I am greatly pleased with your account of Fanny; I found her in the summer just what you describe, almost another Sister, – & could not have supposed that a neice would ever have been so much to me.'

This visit of Cassandra's to Godmersham ended tragically. On 28 September Elizabeth's eleventh child, Brook John, was safely born. On 10 October, Elizabeth died.

Edward's eldest sons, Edward and George, were at school at Winchester. James brought them to Steventon and then sent them on to Southampton where they arrived perished with cold, having travelled on the outside of the coach with no greatcoats. Jane cosseted them and saw to their needs, spiritual and physical. Mrs James had got them each a suit of mourning; but they were distressed because Mary had not thought black pantaloons necessary, and Jane had the lack supplied – 'one would not have them made uncomfortable by the want of what is usual on such occasions.' She played bilbocatch with them (this is cup-and-ball, at which Jane was famously adroit) and spillikins and riddles and conundrums and cards, and encouraged George to make paper boats and shoot them down with horse-chestnuts: she took them on the river, and she took them to church and on Sunday evening they read the Psalms and Lessons and a sermon at home – 'to which they

Stoneleigh Abbey, in 1806 inherited from Lord Leigh by Mrs Austen's cousin, the Rev. Thomas Leigh

Castle Square, Southampton, immediately inside the ramparts

Houses in St Michael's Place,
Brompton; from 1805 to 1809
Henry and Eliza Austen lived at
No. 16

A phaeton and two. 'I am just
returned from my airing in the very
bewitching Phaeton and four.'
(*Letter* from JA to Cassandra,
27 May 1801)

Winchester College, where James's
son Edward and Edward's sons
Edward and George went to school

were very attentive; but you will not expect to hear that they did not return to conundrums the moment it *was over*.'

Before this unhappy event, new family plans had been brewing. Mrs Austen and her daughters, together with Martha Lloyd, had decided to leave Southampton and set up on their own, and various possibilities had been put forward. Edward had offered two houses, one in Kent near Godmersham, and one in Hampshire at Chawton, near his own house Chawton Manor. It was the latter offer that was accepted – after all, they were 'Hampshire-born Austens'.

Removal to Chawton

Chawton was and is a small village on the westerly outskirts of Alton on the Winchester road. The house that Edward offered his mother and sisters was in effect a large cottage said to have been once a posting-inn, more recently occupied by the Chawton Manor steward. It is now known as Chawton Cottage, but that was not its original name, and we do not know what it was called in Jane Austen's day. Dr R. W. Chapman has suggested it was probably the Small House, in distinction to Chawton Manor, which was spoken of in the family as the Great House; and, with Trollope's Small House at Allington in mind, the suggestion seems as likely as any other.

Sir John Moore and his troops in Spain

68

Jane Austen obviously looked forward to the Chawton plan with an enthusiasm quite different from her former determination to make the best of Bath. To old Mrs Knight's hint that she might find a husband in the bachelor Rector of Chawton, she responded flippantly 'she may depend upon it, that I *will* marry Mr. Papillon, whatever may be his reluctance or my own.' 'Yes, yes, we *will* have a pianoforte, as good a one as can be got for thirty guineas,' she wrote to Cassandra at the end of 1808, 'and I will practise country dances, that we may have some amusement for our nephews and nieces' – this time, unusually, she spelt 'nieces' in the now established manner – 'when we have the pleasure of their company.'

For everyone hoped that the move to Chawton might mean a more united family life than had been possible of recent years. It was not far from Steventon, the home of the nieces Anna and Caroline and the nephew Edward. The older Edward, Jane's brother, was clearly intending to spend more time at Chawton Manor; probably Godmersham, after his wife's death, had lost its pleasures, but until 1812 Chawton Manor was let to the Middletons. Frank, whose family was steadily increasing, was engaged early in 1809 in helping fetch off Sir John Moore's army from the Peninsula: 'I wish Sir John had united something of the Christian

◀ The Chawton cottage today

Jane Austen by her sister Cassandra. 'This disappointing sketch', wrote Dr Chapman, 'is the only delineation of Jane Austen's features that can claim authenticity.' When Edward Austen-Leigh decided to have it engraved for his Memoir, his sister, half-sister and cousins gave it only 'very guarded and qualified approval . . . perhaps it gave some idea of the truth.'

with the Hero in his death,' Jane Austen wrote. It is hard for a sailor's family to settle, but Frank was to spend some time at Chawton Manor, and later to live at Alton. Moreover, there were hopes that Charles, who had been almost all this time in the Americas, might soon come home. The family was eagerly waiting to welcome his wife, Frances Palmer, the daughter of the Attorney-General of Bermuda, whom he had married in 1807. But two of their three children had been born before they finally came home in 1811.

The High Street, Alton

Early in 1809 Cassandra left Southampton for Godmersham, and was the first of the family to visit the Chawton cottage. In April Mrs Austen and Jane also left for Godmersham, with a visit to Great Bookham on the way, but before they went Jane Austen wrote a letter which suggests that her mind was turning again to her proper work. Under the pseudonym of Mrs Ashton Dennis she wrote to the publisher Crosby reminding him that in 1803 he had bought a MS. novel called *Susan* for £10. Had it been lost? In this case the Authoress could supply another copy. Or, if Mr Crosby ignored this 'address' she would feel at liberty to try to secure the publication of her work elsewhere. Mr Crosby wrote back curtly. He had the manuscript, but he made no stipulations as to its publication. If anyone else tried to publish it, he would take proceedings. The Authoress might have it back 'for the same as we paid for it.'

There, for the moment, the matter rested. Presumably Jane Austen had not, at this time, £10 to spare. As it happened, an anonymous novel of the same name *was* published this year, which may help to explain why Jane Austen's *Susan* eventually changed her name.

Chawton Manor, near Alton, the Hampshire seat of Edward Austen (after 1812, Knight) and still in the possession of the Knight family

In July 1809 Mrs Austen with her daughters and Martha Lloyd moved into the Chawton cottage. Edward Austen-Leigh, who remembered it well, has given us a description of it:

> A good-sized entrance and two sitting-rooms made the length of the house, all intended originally to look upon the road, but the large drawing-room window was blocked up and turned into a book-case, and another opened at the side which gave to view only turf and trees, as a high wooden fence and hornbeam hedge shut out the Winchester road, which skirted the whole length of the little domain. Trees were planted each side to form a shrubbery walk, carried round the enclosure, which gave a sufficient space for ladies' exercise. There was a pleasant irregular mixture of hedgerow, and gravel walk, and orchard, and long grass for mowing. . . .

In the left-hand parlour, the larger one, stood the piano. The right-hand parlour was the common sitting-room, and there, on a table, lay Jane's mahogany writing-desk; the Austen girls shared a bedroom here, and had no private 'dressing-room' as they had had at Steventon. So it was in the common sitting-room that Jane Austen was to work at her novels, her only protection a creaking door which she begged to have left untended since it gave warning of approach, and an opportunity to slip her manuscript sheets under the blotting-book before anyone came in.

Jane Austen's Music Books: 'Elizabeth is very cruel about my writing music, and, as a punishment for her, I should insist upon always writing out all hers in future, if I were not punishing myself at the same time.' (*Letter* from JA to Cassandra, 8 January 1799)

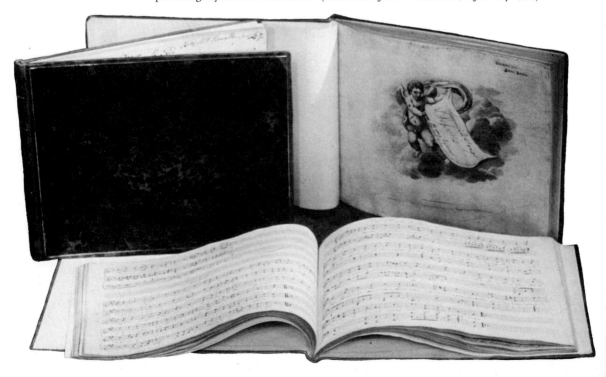

Collier's London–Winchester Coach. 'I want to get rid of some of my things & therefore shall send down a parcel by Collier.' (*Letter* from J A to Cassandra, 17 October 1815)

Situated as it was on the main London–Portsmouth road, the house was inevitably a noisy one, but the family enjoyed the cheerful bustle, and Mrs Austen liked to spend an hour or two at the dining-room window in the mornings, watching the traffic go by. A gentleman who knew old Mrs Knight and had passed the door in a post-chaise wrote to her that he had seen through the window the family 'looking very comfortable at breakfast.'

Very comfortable at Chawton they undoubtedly were. On 26 July 1809, Jane Austen sent her brother Frank some verses on the pleasures of the new home:

> – *Cassandra's pen will paint our state,*
> *The many comforts that await*
> *Our Chawton home, how much we find*
> *Already in it, to our mind;*
> *And how convinced, that when complete*
> *It will all other Houses beat –*

After this, we have no letters until 1811, but this gap is due rather to pleasure than to disaster. As Jane Austen had hoped, the nephews and nieces were often at the cottage, and several have left us recollections of their aunt Jane and the life there.

'My Aunt Jane Austen' 'As to my Aunt's personal appearance,' wrote Caroline, in her loving ill-spelt reminiscences published as *My Aunt Jane Austen*, 'her's was the first face that I can remember thinking pretty. . . . Her face was rather round than long – she had a bright, but not a pink colour – a clear brown complexion and very good hazle eyes. . . . Her hair, a darkish brown, curled naturally – it was in short curls round her face (for *then* ringlets were *not*). She always wore a cap – Such was the custom with the ladies who were not quite young – at least of a morning but I never saw her without one. . . . I beleive my two Aunts were not accounted very good dressers, and were thought to have taken to the garb of middle age unnecessarily soon.'

Detail of patchwork quilt made by Mrs Austen with assistance from Cassandra and Jane. 'Have you remembered to collect peices for the Patchwork? – We are now at a stand still.' (*Letter* from JA to Cassandra, 17 October 1815)

The engraved portrait of Jane Austen which
appeared in Edward Austen‑Leigh's
Memoir, published in 1870 (see illustration
and caption, p. 71)

But it has to be remembered that when Jane Austen left Steventon she was a
young twenty‑five, delighting in clothes and social gaieties. When she came to
Hampshire, after the dreary disappointed years at Bath, she *was* middle‑aged,
nearly thirty‑four years old. Her interest in dances was now rather for James's
Anna and Edward's Fanny than for herself, and the housekeeping she had
attempted with youthful gusto at Steventon was now a serious pursuit, for Mrs
Austen, in a round green smock‑frock, was devoting herself to the garden. The
pretty miniscule sewing of Steventon had developed into a talent for beautiful
embroidery, for Jane Austen was unusually neat‑fingered. 'Her handwriting
remains to bear testimony to its own excellence,' Caroline says, 'and every note and

letter of hers, was finished off handsomely – There was an art *then* in folding and sealing – no adhesive envelopes made all easy – some people's letters looked always loose and untidy – but *her* paper was sure to take the right folds, and *her* sealing wax to drop in the proper place.' She had, we are told, an unusually pretty speaking voice, and in it she would tell made-up stories to the children, until they grew old enough to start writing in their turn and bring their manuscripts to their aunt for criticism.

In view of the frequent malice of the letters, the piercingly cold observation of the novels, Caroline's comments on her aunt's disposition are of interest: ' – my Aunt Jane had a regard for her neighbours and felt a kindly interest in their proceedings. . . . They sometimes served for her amusement, but it was her own nonsense that gave zest to the gossip – She never turned *them* into ridicule – She was as far as possible from being censorious or satirical', and, she says, 'Her charm to children was great sweetness of manner – she seemed to love you, and you loved her naturally in return.'

But despite the time that Jane Austen gave to the children and to her domestic duties, which included sewing for and visiting the poor as she had at Steventon, at Chawton she was writing again. By 1811, *Sense and Sensibility*, a revision of the earlier *Elinor and Marianne*, was ready for publication and had been sold to Thomas Egerton, of the Military Library, Whitehall. He was to publish at his own expense, but the Authoress was to reimburse him for any loss. Probably in

'Mansfield Park' February of this year she had started *Mansfield Park*, but inevitably it was *Sense and Sensibility* that was on her mind. The proofs had started to arrive in April, when she was staying at 64 Sloane Street with Henry and Eliza; and to Cassandra's inquiry as to whether she was too much occupied to think of her forthcoming book, she replied, 'No indeed, I am never too busy to think of S & S. I can no more forget it, than a mother can forget her sucking child.'

Still, there was plenty to do in London, what with shopping and walks and drives and visits to picture exhibitions and to the theatre – Jane Austen was disappointed to miss Mrs Siddons owing to a misunderstanding over dates of performances. And on the occasion of this visit Eliza gave a grand party for sixty-six people which was reported in the *Morning Post* of 25 April. The rooms were dressed with flowers, a glass was lent for the mantelpiece, their own not being yet ready, and music was provided by harp and pianoforte and singers including 'one female singer, a short Miss Davis all in blue.' It was hoped that some of the invited company would contribute to the entertainment, but no amateur could be persuaded to perform.

From Sloane Street Jane Austen seems to have gone on to Streatham, as she and Cassandra often did, to visit their friend, the former Catherine Bigg, now married to the Rector of Streatham, the Rev. Herbert Hill, the father-in-law of Southey's

Pencil portrait by Jane Austen of her favourite niece Fanny, ▶
Edward Austen's eldest daughter

Mrs Siddons as Lady Macbeth; but 'I have no chance of seeing
Mrs Siddons. – She *did* act on Monday, but as Henry was told by
the Boxkeeper that he did not think she would, the places, & all thought
of it, were given up.' (*Letter* from JA to Cassandra, 25 April 1811)

Above left, fashionable linen-draper in Pall Mall

Left, Wedgwood & Byerley's Warehouse in York Street,
St James's Square. 'On Monday I had the pleasure of receiving,
unpacking & approving our Wedgwood ware. It all came very
safely, & upon the whole is a good match.' (*Letter* from JA to
Cassandra, 6 June 1811) Some of this china is still intact at Chawton

daughter. Perhaps it was through him that Jane Austen's novels were introduced to the Lake poets. We learn from Sara Coleridge in 1834 that 'My uncle Southey and my father had an equally high opinion of her merits, but Mr. Wordsworth used to say that though he admitted that her novels were an admirable copy of life, he could not be interested in productions of that kind; unless the truth of nature were presented to him clarified, as it were, by the pervading light of imagination, it had scarce any attractions in his eyes.'

'Sense and Sensibility' Published

Sense and Sensibility: a Novel. In three volumes. By a Lady came out in November 1811, at 15s., and was reasonably well received and successful. So far from Jane Austen having to bear the publisher's losses – Henry tells us 'She actually made a reserve from her very moderate income to meet the expected loss' – she made £140 on a first edition estimated at between 700 and 1,000 copies, which sold out in twenty months. Soon after publication, on 25 November, Lady Bessborough was writing to Lord Granville Leveson Gower, '*Have you read Sense and Sensibility?* It is a clever novel. They were full of it at Althorpe, and tho' it ends stupidly, I was much amused by it.'

The identity of the author was, as far as possible, kept secret. Fanny Austen had received a letter from her Aunt Cassandra in September begging her not to mention that it was her Aunt Jane who had written *Sense and Sensibility*. And Anna knew so little about it, that one day at the circulating library at Alton with Aunt Jane, she picked up *Sense and Sensibility* from the counter, then flung it down again, declaring that with such a title, it must be rubbish.

Whitehall, where Thomas Egerton's
Military Library was situated;
he was Jane Austen's first publisher

Streatham Common. 'I shall leave
Sloane St. on the 1st or 2nd . . . Eliza
talks kindly of conveying me to
Streatham' – where the Rev. Herbert
Hill lived with his wife Catherine,
née Bigg. (*Letter* from JA to
Cassandra, 18 April 1811)

Mrs Leigh Perrot. The Rev. Thomas Leigh, who had inherited Stoneleigh Abbey, died in 1813. 'Poor Mrs L.P. – who would have been Mistress of Stoneleigh had there been none of that vile compromise' – see p. 62. (*Letter* from JA to Francis Austen, 3 July 1813) The estate was inherited by a nephew

In April of the following year, 1812, Mrs Austen and Jane went to stay at Steventon, a visit which Mrs Austen decided should be the last she would ever make; henceforth she would stay in her own home. Old Mrs Knight died in October, and thereafter Edward changed his surname from Austen to Knight.

Such changes, or hyphenating, of names on inheritance of property were then common. The father of Edward's adoptive father had been born Thomas Brodnax; on inheriting Godmersham he became Thomas May; in 1738 he inherited the estate of Knight of Chawton and became Thomas Knight. Again, Mr Leigh Perrot was plain Mr Leigh until in 1774 he inherited Perrot property; and when James Austen's son Edward inherited from Mr Leigh Perrot's widow in 1837, he changed his surname to Austen-Leigh. So it was nothing out of the way that Edward Austen should become Edward Knight: 'I must learn to make a better K,' wrote his sister Jane.

Though she had been working on *Mansfield Park*, the next novel ready for publication was another revision, this time of the earlier *First Impressions*, now renamed *Pride and Prejudice*; the title was almost certainly taken from the last paragraph of Fanny Burney's *Camilla* where the phrase is three times repeated. The revisions were probably substantial; indeed it has been suggested that the original may well have been in the form of letters. Certainly at some stage the novel was longer than it is, for Jane Austen wrote to Cassandra: 'I have lop't and crop't so successfully, however, that I imagine it must be shorter than S. & S. altogether.' Here she was wrong; it was not. Finally revised to her satisfaction, the newly made novel was, in November 1812, sold to Egerton for £110.

Pride and Prejudice: A novel. In three volumes. By the Author of 'Sense and Sensibility' was published by Egerton on 29 January 1813, at 18*s*., in an edition of about 1,500 copies. On that day Jane Austen wrote an excited letter to Cassandra, devoting almost all her space to the great event:

> I want to tell you that I have got my own darling child from London. . . . The Advertisement is in our paper to-day for the first time 18ˢ. He shall ask £1.1 for my two next & £1.8 for my stupidest of all. . . . Miss Benn [a neighbour] dined with us on the very day of the books coming & in the evening we set fairly at it, and read half the first vol. to her, prefacing that, having intelligence from Henry that such a work would soon appear, we had desired him to send it whenever it came out, and I believe it passed with her unsuspected. She was amused, poor soul! *That* she could not help, you know, with two such people to lead the way, but she really does seem to admire Elizabeth. I must confess that I think her as delightful a creature as ever appeared in print, and how I shall be able to tolerate those who do not like *her* at least I do not know. . . .

People who do *not* like Elizabeth Bennet must be very few indeed, and Elizabeth Jenkins can justly claim, in her biography of Jane Austen, that 'Elizabeth Bennet

'Mrs Bennet and her two youngest girls'. Illustration to *Pride and Prejudice* by Hugh Thompson for the George Allen edition of 1894

Warren Hastings by Thomas Lawrence: 'I long to have you hear Mr H.'s opinion of P. and P. His admiring my Elizabeth so much is particularly welcome to me.' (*Letter* from JA to Cassandra, 15 September 1813)

Praise has perhaps received more admiration than any other heroine in English Literature.' Robert Louis Stevenson said that when Elizabeth Bennet opened her mouth, he wanted to go down on his knees, and Professor Bradley: 'I am meant to fall in love with her and I do.' Only Sir Walter Scott wryly remarked that it was seeing Pemberley that led Elizabeth Bennet to feel she had made a mistake in rejecting its owner.

The few criticisms Jane Austen herself made of the book do not disguise her delight and satisfaction in it. Granted, but not very seriously granted, the work was 'rather too light, and bright, and sparkling', and wanted shade – 'a long chapter of sense, if it could be had; it not, of solemn specious nonsense, about something unconnected with the story; an essay on writing, a critique on Walter Scott, or the history of Buonaparté, or anything that would form a contrast, and bring the reader with increased delight to the playfulness and epigrammatism of the general style.'

The reception was good. In the larger world Richard Brinsley Sheridan advised a Miss Shirreff to buy it immediately, for it was one of the cleverest things he had read, and Miss Annabella Milbanke, who was to marry Lord Byron in 1815, wrote to her mother that she thought *Pride and Prejudice* 'a very superior work . . . the *most probable* fiction I have ever read. It is not a crying book, but the interest is very strong, especially for Mr. Darcy.' Enough people shared their opinions for the first edition to be sold out by July and a second one published in November,

Sir Walter Scott by Edwin Landseer. 'Read again, and for the third time at least, Miss Austen's very finely written novel of Pride and Prejudice . . . The Big Bow-wow strain I can do myself like any now going; but the exquisite touch, which renders ordinary commonplace things and characters interesting, from the truth of the description and the sentiment, is denied to me.' (Journal, 14 and 28 March 1837)

together with a second edition of *Sense and Sensibility*. By July, Jane Austen was able to tell Frank that she had written herself into £250 – 'which only makes me long for more.'

Nearer home, Fanny liked it: 'Fanny's praise is very gratifying. . . . Her liking Darcy & Elizabeth is enough, she might hate all the others if she would.' And Warren Hastings to whom Henry had sent a copy was, it seems, delighted with it.

For the secret of the authorship was leaking out. Already at the beginning of the year there were rumours of it around Chawton, but it was Henry who let it out. As Jane Austen wrote to her brother Frank:

– the truth is that the Secret has spread so far as to be scarcely the Shadow of a secret now – & that I beleive whenever the 3^d appears, I shall not even attempt to tell Lies about it. – I shall rather try to make all the Money than all the Mystery I can of it. – People shall pay for their knowledge if I can make them. – Henry heard P. & P. warmly praised in Scotland, by Lady Robt Kerr & another Lady; – & what does he do in the warmth of his Brotherly vanity & Love, but immediately tell them who wrote it! A Thing once set going in that way – one knows how it spreads! – and he, dear Creature, has set it going so much more than once. I know it is all done from affection & partiality

Jane Austen would forgive anything to her favourite Henry, and perhaps the more so in that 1813, a year of triumph for her, was a difficult one for him. On

87

Spring Gardens in Pimlico, London. 'Henry & I went to the Exhibition in Spring Gardens. It is not thought a good collection, but I was very well pleased.' (*Letter* from JA to Cassandra, 24 May 1813)

Below right, an exhibition of water-coloured drawings. 'We have been both to the exhibition & Sir J. Reynolds' . . . I had great amusement among the pictures.' (*Letter* from JA to Francis Austen, 25 September 1813)

25 April, his wife Eliza had died – a loss, though not, it appears, so terrible a loss as might have been expected. As Jane put it, 'his Mind is not a Mind for affliction. He is too Busy, too active, too sanguine', and poor Eliza had been ill for a long time. Still, some shock must have been sustained, and probably the bilious attacks from which he suffered badly that year were part of the price he paid. All the same, when Jane stayed with him in Sloane Street in May, the time seems to have passed pleasantly enough, and one of its pleasures was a visit to an exhibition of paintings in Spring Gardens, where Jane was delighted to find 'a small portrait of Mrs. Bingley, excessively like her. I went in hopes of seeing one of her Sister, but there was no Mrs. Darcy.' She hoped to find Mrs Darcy at another, the 'great Exhibition', or perhaps at Sir Joshua Reynolds' exhibition, but she was not at either: 'I can only imagine that Mr. D. prizes any Picture of her too much to like it should be exposed to the public eye. – I can imagine he w^d have that sort of feeling – that mixture of Love, Pride & Delicacy.'

For Jane Austen, then, her characters' lives continued far beyond the limits of the novels in which she confined them, and she would often tell her family of what happened to them after the novels were finished. So we know that Miss Steele, of *Sense and Sensibility*, did *not* catch the Doctor, that Kitty Bennet married a clergy-man at Pemberley, and her sister Mary, one of Uncle Philips's clerks.

Family Visits　　Henry gave up the house in Sloane Street and went to live above his offices at 10 Henrietta Street, and in September Jane went to stay with him there. There was something of a family party in London at the time, for Edward was up with some of his children on such duties as visits to the dentist. Fanny stayed in Henrietta Street with Henry and Jane, and there was time for plenty of shopping and theatre-going before Jane went off with the Knights for what was to be a last visit to Godmersham, for the Knights were spending more and more time at Chawton Manor and were eventually to move there altogether. While at Godmersham they had the pleasure (though it seems to have been a modified pleasure) of a visit from Charles and his wife and children. He was commanding the *Namur*, the guardship at the Nore, and his family was living on board with him, though little Cassy, his eldest, was sadly seasick whenever it was rough. In that autumn of 1813 James's Anna, now aged eighteen, became engaged to Ben Lefroy, brother of the then Rector of Ashe and son of Jane Austen's dear friend. Anna had made another engagement earlier in the year, to a Mr Michael Terry, but it had been broken off, and the family was well satisfied with this new one.

Benjamin Lefroy (1791–1829). 'I beleive he is sensible, certainly very religious' – he was not yet in orders – 'well connected & with some Independance.' (*Letter* from JA to Francis Austen, 25 September 1813)

Henrietta Street, Covent Garden. 'I then walked into No. 10, which is all dirt and confusion, but in a very promising way.' (*Letter* from J A to Cassandra, 24 May 1813)

Through all this full and interesting period of family life Jane Austen had been writing *Mansfield Park* – from 'somewhere about Feb^{ry}' until 'soon after June 1813', according to her own account, and now and again she refers to it in her letters. 'If you could discover whether Northamptonshire is a country of Hedgerows I should be glad again,' she wrote to Cassandra, but whatever incident was to be founded on hedgerows failed to appear. Of Frank in July she asked, 'shall you object to my mentioning the Elephant in it, & two or three other of your old Ships?' Frank did not object, and the ships were duly mentioned.

Writing 'Mansfield Park'

91

An author is not necessarily the best witness to the purport of his or her own work, but it is, at first sight, surprising to find Jane Austen telling her sister that this new novel was to be of 'a complete change of subject – ordination.' Some critics have supposed the 'change of subject' to refer to something other than the work in progress, and they may be right. Yet, if we read the novel with this possible intention in mind, it does not seem unreasonable to accept ordination as the novelist's intended subject. To set with her celebrated praise of the Navy in *Persuasion*, we have in Chapter IX of the first volume of *Mansfield Park* a eulogium of the country clergyman. We learn what his attitude should be to a family living

'Admiral Croft'. Illustration to *Persuasion* by Hugh
Thompson for the Macmillan edition of 1897

'Seized up in the Rigging'. A naval picture of 1818

waiting for his acceptance, and to non-residence, and of the importance of good sermons and a clear delivery, all subjects that must constantly have been discussed in the Austen family. For even in those days when the Church was one of only a few professions open to a poor gentleman or a younger son, Jane Austen had surely an unusually large number of relations and friends in Holy Orders. Her father was a clergyman and so, eventually, were two of her brothers. Her sister was engaged to a clergyman and so, it seems, might she have been herself had death not supervened. The father of the Lloyd girls was a clergyman and so were two of their husbands – and this is only to scratch the surface of the circumambient clergy.

It is true that in so far as *Mansfield Park* is a novel about ordination, this material is less well integrated into the story than, say, the matter of the private theatricals. 'In a *general* light private theatricals are open to some objections', Edmund Bertram says gravely to his brother. This may seem surprising when we remember how much private theatricals were enjoyed in the Austen family in the 1780s, but we often forget to what an extent opinions or morals were changing during, roughly, the Regency period (1810–20) from what we tend to think of as Georgian to what we think of as Victorian, and largely under the influence of Evangelical religion. 'I do not like the Evangelicals,' Jane Austen had written in 1809, but in 1814, 'I am by no means convinced that we ought not all to be Evangelicals.' And her change in attitude to private theatricals can be paralleled by a not dissimilar change in her near-contemporary Dorothy Wordsworth who, in her tour in Scotland in 1822, was apologizing for the casual Sunday travelling of her earlier tour in 1803.

In March 1814 Jane Austen was driving to London with her brother Henry, and when they reached the village of Bentley Green a little to the west of Farnham, she began to read *Mansfield Park* aloud to him and continued until they reached the marriage of Mrs Rushworth. 'Henry's approbation hitherto is even equal to my wishes,' Jane wrote to Cassandra, and later, as Henry continued reading in Henrietta Street, 'He admires H. Crawford: I mean properly, as a clever, pleasant man.'

Publication of 'Mansfield Park'

Mansfield Park: A Novel. In three volumes. By the Author of 'Sense and Sensibility', and 'Pride and Prejudice' was published by Egerton in May 1814 at 18s., and the first edition of some 1,500 copies was sold out in six months. Jane Austen collected the opinions of family and friends on *Mansfield Park* and later on *Emma*, so we know that Mr and Mrs Cooke of Great Bookham were very much pleased 'with the Manner in which the Clergy are treated', that Anna could not bear Fanny, that Fanny Knight wanted 'more Love between her & Edmund' and that Mr Egerton the publisher 'praised it for it's Morality, & for being so equal a Composition. – No weak parts.' In general the family thought very well of it, though most of them retained a preference for *Pride and Prejudice*.

94

'A Sleepy Congregation' by Thomas Rowlandson. 'We do not much like Mr Cooper's new Sermons; – they are fuller of Regeneration & Conversion than ever.' (*Letter* from JA to Cassandra, 8 September 1816)

Scene from David Garrick's comedy *The Clandestine Marriage*, by John Zoffany. 'Fanny and the two little girls are gone to take places for to-night at Covent Garden: "Clandestine Marriage" and "Midas".' (*Letter* from JA to Cassandra, 15 September 1813)

Jane Anna Elizabeth Lefroy
(1793–1872), elder daughter of
James Austen

As is usual with novels, many people, both eventually and contemporaneously, have sought for real-life correspondences in Jane Austen's novels. Was casual debonair Henry Crawford taken from Henry Austen, they ask, or Mary Crawford, who didn't want to marry a clergyman, from Henry Austen's wife Eliza? In Austen family tradition, William Price, with his boldness, his brotherly affection and his love of dancing, was taken from the younger sailor brother, Charles, while among the opinions of the book that Jane Austen collected was that of a Mrs Bramstone who thought Lady Bertram like herself. In fact, correspondences can seldom be as exact as those surmises would have them, but there is, in *Mansfield Park*, one object that we can be reasonably sure was taken from life, and this is the gold and amber cross that William Price brought from Sicily for his sister Fanny; for in 1801 Charles Austen, stationed in the Mediterranean, had sent home gold chains and topaz crosses for his sisters, bought out of an unexpected bounty of prize money.

'Emma'   On 21 January 1814 Jane Austen began *Emma*. 'I am going to take a heroine whom no one but myself will much like,' she said. But it was not only her own novel to which her attention was given. Anna, who in November 1814 became Anna Lefroy at what must, by all accounts, have been a charming family wedding at Steventon, had taken seriously to novel-writing too, and Jane Austen's criticisms to Anna reveal some of the principles that guided her own work.

96

Captain Charles Austen
(1779–1852)

Her most constant suggestions tend always to be demands for probability and accuracy. 'I have scratched out Sir Tho: from walking with the other Men to the Stables &c the very day after his breaking his arm – for though I find your Papa *did* walk out immediately after *his* arm was set, I think it can be so little usual as to *appear* unnatural in a book. . . . I have also scratched out the Introduction between Lord P. & his Brother, & Mr. Griffin. A Country Surgeon (dont tell Mr. C. Lyford) would not be introduced to Men of their rank'; and again 'we [that is, Cassandra and herself] think you had better not leave England. Let the Portmans go to Ireland, but as you know nothing of the Manners there, you had better not go with them. You will be in danger of giving false representations. Stick to Bath & the Foresters. There you will be quite at home.' 'Devereux Forester's being ruined by his Vanity is extremely good,' she writes later, 'but I wish you would not let him plunge into a "vortex of Dissipation." I do not object to the Thing, but I cannot bear the expression; – it is such thorough novel slang – and so old, that I dare say Adam met with it in the first novel he opened.' She is, however, enchanted with Anna's invented name of Newton-Priors – 'It is delightful. – One could live upon the name of Newton-Priors for a twelvemonth.' 'You are now collecting your People delightfully,' she writes, 'getting them exactly into such a spot as is the delight of my life; – 3 or 4 Families in a Country Village is the very thing to work on.'

No. 22 Hans Place; Henry Austen moved to
No. 23 in 1814. 'It is a delightful Place . . . & the
Garden is quite a Love. I am in the front Attic,
which is the Bedchamber to be preferred.'
(*Letter* from JA to Cassandra, August, 1814)

Jane Austen's publisher, John Murray, in the
Drawing-room at 50 Albemarle Street, in 1815
(below)

Not only Anna's novel but also the love affairs of her favourite niece Fanny demanded Jane Austen's attention that year. Was Fanny really in love with Mr Plumtree? Her aunt assured her that she wasn't. – 'I have no scruple in saying that you cannot be in Love. . . . What strange creatures we are! – It seems as if your being secure of him (as you say yourself) had made you Indifferent. . . . Poor dear Mr. J.P.! – Oh! dear Fanny, your mistake has been one that thousands of women fall into. He was the *first* young Man who attached himself to you. That was the charm, & most powerful it is.' 'Anything', she assures Fanny, 'is to be preferred or endured rather than marrying without Affection . . . it is no creed of mine, as you must be well aware, that such sort of Disappointments kill anybody.' She kept Fanny's confidences private, even from Cassandra.

Henry, who was now Receiver-General for Oxfordshire, had moved at mid-summer from Henrietta Street to 23 Hans Place, and there Jane visited him in November, and also visited Anna and Ben Lefroy who were living at Hendon; she wrote to Fanny of Anna's happiness and of her extravagance: she had bought a violet pelisse and a 24-guinea piano. Charles's wife had died of her fourth baby in September, and Jane went to see his orphaned little girls who were being looked after in Keppel Street, off Russell Square.

Edward Knight that year had been engaged with a lawsuit. His income from Godmersham was already £5,000 a year, but Chawton, which brought in £10,000, was being claimed by another member of the Knight family. The case dragged on, and was not settled in Edward's favour until 1818.

His sister Jane, on her own scale, had also been thinking about money. Would Egerton venture a second edition of *Mansfield Park*? 'People are more ready to borrow & praise, than to buy – which I cannot wonder at; – but tho' I like praise as well as anybody, I like what Edward calls *Pewter* too.' It was probably to some extent the pursuit of pewter that led Jane Austen to change her publisher. *Emma* was offered to Mr John Murray of Albemarle Street. His reader, William Gifford, editor of the *Quarterly Review*, wrote that of *Emma* he had 'nothing but good to say', and Mr Murray proposed to pay £450 for the copyrights of *Sense and Sensibility*, *Mansfield Park* and *Emma*. Henry Austen pointed out that his sister had made more

A Moor Park apricot. 'It was only the spring twelve month before Mr. Norris's death, that we put in the apricot . . . it's a moor park, we bought it as a moor park.' (Mrs Norris in *Mansfield Park*, Ch. VI. Vol. I)

out of 'one very moderate edition of *Mansfield Park* (you yourself expressed astonishment that so small an edition of such a work should have been sent into the world) and a still smaller one of *Sense and Sensibility*.' Eventually Mr Murray agreed to publish a first edition of *Emma* and a second edition of *Sense and Sensibility* on profit-sharing terms. Jane Austen said of her new publisher, 'He is a rogue of course, but a civil one.'

In October 1815, before *Emma* was published, Henry fell ill of one of his bilious attacks, which this time turned to a serious illness. Jane was in London with him at the time, and the strain his illness imposed on her appears to have begun the undermining of her own health; but at the time it was to other things that Henry's illness directly led. For his surgeon, an excellent young man called Charles Haden, *Royal Favour* was acquainted with one of the doctors of the Prince Regent. The Prince, he was able to tell Jane, was an admirer of her works, and kept a set of them in every one of his residences, and it was through Mr Haden's reporting that Miss Jane Austen was in town that she received a visit from the Rev. James Stanier Clarke, the Prince's domestic chaplain. Mr Clarke took Jane Austen to see the splendours of Carlton House, the Prince's residence, and then intimated to her that the dedication of her new book to the Prince would not be found inacceptable.

Only a couple of years earlier, Jane Austen had written of Queen Caroline, 'Poor woman, I shall support her as long as I can, because she *is* a woman and because I hate her husband.' But royal favour is apt to dazzle. *Emma* was 'most respectfully dedicated' to his Royal Highness the Prince Regent 'by His Royal Highness's dutiful and obedient humble servant The Author', and Jane Austen arranged with Mr Murray that the presentation copies should be specially bound in scarlet with the Prince of Wales's feathers on the spine.

Emma, specially bound
for the Prince Regent

The Prince Regent
driving a curricle, by
Thomas Rowlandson

The Crimson Drawing-
room at Carlton House

H.R.H. the Princess Charlotte Augusta
(1796–1817), only child of the Prince Regent

Prince Leopold of Saxe-Coburg-Saalfeld,
who married Princess Charlotte in May, 1816

Mr Clarke, however, became something of a nuisance. Would Miss Jane Austen consider, he asked, in some future work delineating 'the Habits of Life and Character and enthusiasm of a Clergyman'? Miss Jane Austen would not. 'A classical education . . . appears to me quite indispensable for the person who would do any justice to your clergyman; and I think I may boast myself to be, with all possible vanity, the most unlearned and uninformed female who ever dared to be an authoress.' Mr Clarke was not deterred. He enlarged on the clergyman he had in mind, who seemed to bear some singular resemblances to himself, and, when this proposal still failed to meet with any response, suggested an 'historical romance, illustrative of the history of the august House of Coburg', which might be dedicated to Prince Leopold of Coburg, then about to marry the Regent's daughter, Princess Charlotte. Again Jane Austen refused: 'I could no more write a romance than an epic poem. I could not sit seriously down to write a serious romance under any other motive than to save my life; and if it were indispensable for me to keep it up and never relax into laughing at myself or other people, I am sure I should be hung before I had finished the first chapter.' The correspondence lapsed.

Emma: A Novel. In three volumes. By the Author of 'Pride and Prejudice', &c. &c. was published in December 1815 (but dated 1816) at 21*s*. The first edition was of some 2,000 copies, of which about 1,200 were sold within the year. Generally the reception was excellent. Sir Walter Scott's review appeared in the *Quarterly* the following March and was such as to delight the author, though she regretted that among his comments on her other novels, he had ignored *Mansfield Park*. Mr Jeffrey, of the *Edinburgh Review*, admitted to having been kept up three nights by it. Jane Austen sent a presentation copy to Maria Edgeworth; not only had Miss Edgeworth's father been a neighbour of the Leigh Perrots in Berkshire, but, as Jane Austen had written to Anna in 1814, 'I have made up my mind to like no Novels really, but Miss Edgeworth's, Yours & my own.' It is fortunate that she could not read Miss Edgeworth's letter to her brother: 'There was no story in it,

Maria Edgeworth (1767–1849). She thought far less well of *Emma* than the author could have hoped

105

View of Box Hill, Surrey

except that Miss Emma found that the man whom she designed for Harriet's lover was an admirer of her own – & he was affronted by being refused by Emma & Harriet wore the willow – and *smooth, thin water-gruel* is according to Emma's father's opinion a very good thing & it is very difficult to make a cook understand what you mean by *smooth thin water-gruel!*'

Almost everything, sooner or later, in one form or another, is grist to the writer's mill. The visits to Great Bookham had provided the knowledge of Box Hill, the venue of the celebrated picnic where Emma was inexcusably rude to Miss Bates.

Leatherhead Church

In near-by Leatherhead, as Miss Elizabeth Jenkins has pointed out, there is a
Randalls Road, and in Leatherhead Church the name of Knightley appears as
a benefactor. But, for all her care, in *Emma* Jane Austen made one bad mistake, as
her brother Edward did not hesitate to point out. 'I should like to know, Jane,'
he said, 'where you got those apple trees of yours that blossom in July?'

As with *Mansfield Park*, Jane Austen collected the opinions of family and
friends on *Emma*, ranging from the enthusiastic to the deprecating. She was, as
always, prepared to tell the family 'what happened next'. The word Frank

Churchill laid before Jane Fairfax, we learn, was 'Pardon'. Mr Woodhouse died two years after Emma's marriage and then she and George Knightley went back to live at Donwell Abbey. Jane Fairfax died nine years after her marriage.

First Translations After *Emma* was published, Henry Austen bought back the manuscript of *Susan* from Crosby. Only after he had done so, did he reveal to Crosby that it was by the author of *Pride and Prejudice*. The year of *Emma*'s publication saw too Jane Austen's first foreign translation: *Raison et Sensibilité, ou les Deux Manières d'Aimer. Traduit librement de l'anglais, par Mme. Isabelle de Montolieu* appeared in Paris in 1815. The next year there appeared in France *Le Parc de Mansfield, ou Les Trois Couisines* and *La Nouvelle Emma, ou les Caractères Anglais du Siècle. Emma* was also published in Philadelphia in 1816.

'Persuasion' According to her own memorandum, Jane Austen began her new novel, *Persuasion*, on 8 August 1815. As Miss Mary Lascelles has put it, 'From the beginning she was accustomed to the pressure of close quarters in a large family whose notions of hospitality were liberal. She learnt how to lead her life unperturbed in a throng' – but still we must marvel that at this stage of her life she managed to do any writing at all. Quite apart from any other social or family duties, she took auntship seriously. 'Now that you are become an Aunt, you are a person of some consequence & must excite great Interest whatever you do. I have always maintained the importance of Aunts as much as possible,' she wrote to Caroline Austen in October 1815, when Caroline's half-sister Anna Lefroy had her first child. That autumn, with all the business of Henry's illness and the bringing out of *Emma*, she had Fanny staying with her in Hans Place, and must chaperon the *tendresse* that arose between her and Mr Haden the surgeon on a social evening with some music from the harp: 'on the opposite side Fanny & Mr. Haden in two chairs (I *believe* at least they had *two* chairs) talking together uninterruptedly.' Anna and Ben Lefroy moved that autumn from Hendon to Wyards, a farmhouse near Alton, and there was Anna's second novel, *Which is the Heroine?* to aid with critical comment; Anna's first novel, *Enthusiasm*, had been abandoned. James Austen's other children were writing too, and must submit their manuscripts to Aunt Jane. Caroline sent her stories and Edward, her future biographer, now on the point of leaving Winchester, had almost inevitably started a novel, which his aunt thought well of, as she did of him himself; 'Edward is a great pleasure to me', she told Cassandra. It was when some of Edward's novel was mislaid that Jane Austen, disavowing theft, wrote to him her famous description of her own work, on 16 December 1816:

'What should I do with your strong, manly, spirited Sketches, full of Variety and Glow? – How could I possibly join them on to the little bit (two Inches wide) of Ivory on which I work with so fine a Brush, as produces little effect after much labour?'

Wyards near Alton, where Ben and Anna Lefroy lived from 1815

In March 1816 the firm of Austen, Maude, and Tilson failed, and Henry Austen went bankrupt, entailing losses to several of the family. Mr Leigh Perrot, who had gone surety for Henry on his appointment as Receiver-General for Oxfordshire, lost £10,000. Some of Edward's money went too, and Jane Austen herself lost £13 of the profits of *Mansfield Park*. Henry, however, was as resilient as ever. He quickly decided to take Orders, began to revise his knowledge of the Greek Testament, and when he was ordained in August surprised the bishop with his erudition. In December he became Curate (in today's nomenclature, Rector) of Bentley, between Alton and Farnham, and an earnest Evangelical preacher. 'Uncle Henry writes very superior Sermons,' Jane Austen wrote to her nephew Edward.

On 18 July 1816, Jane Austen completed her first version of *Persuasion*, but it did not satisfy her. The original tenth chapter was substantially rewritten, and a new eleventh chapter written, the original eleventh chapter becoming, with some small changes, the twelfth. It is universally agreed that this improvement, completed on 6 August, was great, not least because it gives us the only serious love scene Jane Austen ever wrote. Hitherto she had avoided the direct confrontation of lovers at moments of love as she had avoided ever showing us men without the company of women. The notable increase in depth and tenderness of *Persuasion* has led many readers to assume that in it Jane Austen was telling a love story of her own. A Mrs Barrett, who apparently knew Jane Austen, wrote to Edward Austen-Leigh, 'Anne Elliott was herself; her enthusiasm for the navy, and her perfect unselfishness, reflect her completely': and Rudyard Kipling, in his vulgar, loving poem 'Jane's Marriage', went further:

> In a private limbo
>   Where none had thought to look,
> Sat a Hampshire gentleman
>   Reading of a book.
> It was called Persuasion,
>   And it told the plain
> Story of the love between
>   Him and Jane.

But, as we have seen, Jane Austen's love story was *not* that of *Persuasion*; and when we recall that she said to Fanny Knight, 'You may *perhaps* like the Heroine, as she is almost too good for me,' we can see that all intimate guesses are best left aside. It is safer to surmise, if we must, on the part Jane Austen's brother Frank played in the book. He was accused of being the model for Captain Wentworth, but said,

July 8

Chap. 10.

With all this knowledge of Mr. E. & this authority to impart it, Anne left Westgate Buildgs — her mind deeply busy in revolving what she had heard, feeling, thinking, recalling & foreseeing everything; shocked at Mr. Elliot, sighing over future Kellynch, and pained for Lady Russell, [illegible] whose confidence in him had been entire. — The Embarrassment which must be felt from this hour in his presence! — How to behave to him? — how to get rid of him? — What to do by any of the Party at home? — where to be blind? where to be active? — It was altogether a confusion of Images & Doubts — a perplexity, an agitation which she could not see the end of. And she was in Gay St & still so much engrossed, that she started on being addressed by Admd. Croft, as if a person unlikely to be met there.

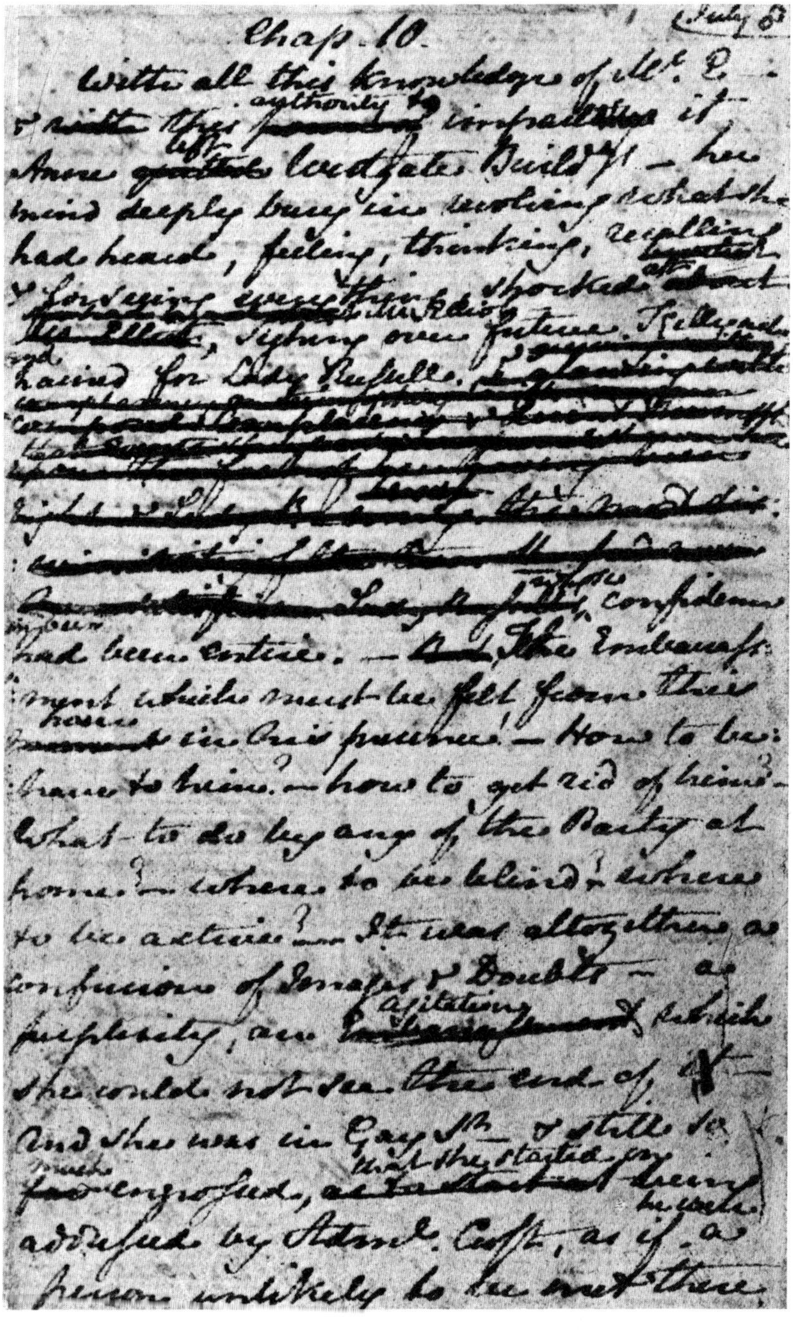

The first page of the cancelled Chapter X of the second volume of *Persuasion*

◀ Bentley, Hampshire, where Henry Austen became Curate in December, 1816

'I rather think that parts of Captain Harville's character were drawn from myself; at least the description of his domestic habits, tastes and occupations have a considerable resemblance to mine.'

'Susan'
Rewritten

Some other writing was undertaken this year. *Susan*, back in its author's hands, was revised, though its new title was not yet decided on; and about this time Jane Austen also drew up the amusing 'Plan of a Novel, according to hints from various quarters', with footnotes indicating what suggestion came from whom.

But though her spirits were high and her inventiveness unflagging, her health was failing. In May 1816 she went to Cheltenham with Cassandra to try the

waters there, but they were not efficacious, and from the end of the year few of her letters fail to refer to her health. In January 1817 she is feeling better. She has walked to Alton; in any case, the weather is unsuitable for the donkey carriage. She becomes convinced that bile is the cause of her trouble, and believes she can ward off any serious return of her illness. In March she means to take to riding instead of driving the donkey, and a ride is actually achieved, with Cassandra and her nephew Edward walking by her side. But she has also fever to report, and bad nights and an ugly complexion – 'I must not depend upon being ever very blooming again. Sickness is a dangerous Indulgence at my time of Life.' *Illness*

The Old Wells and Pump Room, Cheltenham

The death of Uncle Leigh Perrot in April brought on a relapse, even though it had been expected for some time, and in April Jane Austen made her will, leaving everything to Cassandra apart from £50 to Henry and £50 to Madame Bigeon, Henry's French housekeeper whose savings had vanished in his bankruptcy. A later memorandum left a gold chain to her god-daughter Louisa Knight, and a lock of her hair to Fanny.

Now Jane Austen could indulge herself to the extent of making a couch of three chairs to rest on in the family living-room. 'It never looked comfortable,' wrote her niece Caroline, but her Aunt Jane told her that if she ever used the sofa, 'Grandmama would be leaving it for her, and would not lie down, as she did now, whenever she felt inclined.'

The last time Caroline saw her Aunt Jane was in April 1817. She had been staying with Anna, and the sisters walked over to Chawton to inquire after their aunt.

> She was keeping her room but said she would see us, and we went up to her – She was in her dressing gown and was sitting quite like an invalide in an arm chair – but she got up, and kindly greeted us – and then pointing to seats which had been arranged for us by the fire, she said, 'There's a chair for the married lady, and a little stool for you, Caroline.' – It is strange, but those trifling words are the last of her's that I can remember. . . . She was very pale – her voice was weak and low and there was about her, a general appearance of debility and suffering; but I have been told that she never *had* much actual pain.

In an article in the *British Medical Journal* of 18 July 1964, Zachary Cope has diagnosed Jane Austen's symptoms as being those of Addison's disease of the suprarenal capsules, one of the two forms of the disease recognized and distinguished by Addison in 1849. In 1817, with the condition unidentified, there was nothing to be done about it. Eventually Mr Giles King Lyford was called in. He was surgeon-in-ordinary at the county hospital in Winchester, and probably a nephew of Mr John Lyford of Basingstoke who had attended the Austens when they were at Steventon. (John Lyford's son, Charles Lyford, was the 'Country Surgeon' that Jane Austen had referred to, in 1814, in her letter to Anna on etiquette in her novel.)

Winchester Mr Lyford's treatment seemed to do good, and it was decided in May that Jane should go to Winchester to be under his care.

Mrs James Austen lent her carriage for the journey. 'Now that's a sort of thing which Mrs J. Austen does in the kindest manner! – But still she is in the main *not* a liberal-minded Woman', Jane Austen wrote to Anne Sharp, a former governess at Godmersham who had become a friend. Cassandra went with Jane to nurse her, and Henry Austen and young William Knight rode by the carriage, to escort her to lodgings in the house of Mrs David in College Street, Winchester.

Mr William Curtis,
Apothecary at Alton

The lodgings were, Jane said, 'very comfortable. We have a neat little Drawing
room with a Bow-window overlooking Dr. Gabell's garden.' Near by in the
Close lived a good friend, Mrs Heathcote, the former Elizabeth Bigg; her sister
Alethea Bigg, a particular friend of the Austen sisters, lived there with her, but was
away in Switzerland at the time. Jane Austen bore the journey well, and for a time
felt better and sanguine of recovery.

She was still writing, as she had been all the year. In February she had written
several letters to 'dearest Fanny' – James Austen's children rated only 'My dear
Anna' or ' – Edward' or ' – Caroline'. Fanny was in the throes of a new love
affair, this time with a Mr Wildman of Chilham Castle, near Godmersham.

(Overleaf) Winchester High Street. College Street is beyond the Cathedral which is to the right, ▶
below the Butter Cross

My dearest Fanny, You are inimitable, irresistable. You are the delight of my Life. . . . You are the Paragon of all that is Silly & Sensible, common-place & eccentric, Sad & Lively, Provoking & Interesting. . . . Oh! what a loss it will be when you are married. You are too agreable in your single state, too agreable as a Neice. I shall hate you when your delicious play of Mind is all settled down into conjugal & maternal affections.

Not that she is against marriage: 'Single Women have a dreadful propensity for being poor – which is one very strong argument in favour of Matrimony, but I need not dwell on such arguments with *you*, pretty Dear, you do not want inclination.' But there is no need to be in a hurry, and in a later letter to Fanny she refers to Anna Lefroy, now pregnant with her third child: 'Poor Animal, she will be worn out before she is thirty.'

She told Fanny in March that 'Miss Catherine is put upon the Shelve for the present, and I do not know that she will ever come out.' This was the revised *Susan* eventually to appear as *Northanger Abbey*. Jane Austen may well have had qualms about venturing a parody of the Gothick novel some twenty years after *The Mysteries of Udolpho* had been published. 'But,' she added, 'I have a something ready for Publication, which may perhaps appear about a twelvemonth hence.'

'*Northanger Abbey*'

This, of course, was *Persuasion*. But on 17 January 1817, she had, despite her poor health, begun a new novel, which the family believed was to be called *The Brothers*. She dated this work as it went along, and the date on the last quire is 18 March, by which time some 24,000 words had been written. It is a story set against the background of a coastal resort in the throes of development – she may have had the recent exploitation of Bognor in mind – and it eventually became known as *Sanditon*.

Last Novel

It is said that Mr Lyford knew Jane Austen must die, but at first, at Winchester, she still hoped for recovery. She was feeling better, she had been out in a sedan chair and hoped to go out in a wheel chair when the weather improved. She continued to write letters, repeated to little Caroline advice she had often given her: Caroline should not spend so much time on her stories, for she herself had often wished that at Caroline's age she had written less and read more. The day before she died she was writing doggerel verse of abominable scansion about the Winchester races.

But it had become plain that she must soon die, and in July her brothers James and Henry felt it their duty as clergymen to tell her so. She was 'not appalled', but thankful that she had remained in her right mind, and asked them to administer the communion service before she became too weak and wandering to follow it with all her faculties.

A nurse had been got in, but she did not please Cassandra, and Mrs James

Austen came to take her place. 'You have always been a kind sister to me, Mary,'
said Jane. One of her last pleasures was in reading and re-reading Fanny's letters.

On Thursday, 17 July, Cassandra went into the town on some errand for her
sister and found, on returning, that she had had an attack of faintness. It passed off
slightly, but soon returned, and she suffered greatly, crying out, 'God, grant me
patience, Pray for me oh Pray for me!' Cassandra asked her if there was anything
she wanted. She replied that she wanted nothing but death. Mr Lyford came and

was able somewhat to relieve her, but by 7 p.m. she was unconscious and lay perfectly still save for a slight movement of her head with each breath. Cassandra sat by her for six hours, with a pillow on her lap to support Jane's head which was nearly off the bed. Then, for two and a half hours, Mary relieved her. Cassandra came back at 3.30 a.m. and an hour later, on Friday, 18 July, Jane Austen died in her sister's arms. She was forty-two years old.

Jane Austen's Death

She was buried in Winchester Cathedral the following Thursday early in the morning before Morning Service. Cassandra did not attend, nor did Mrs Austen come over from Chawton; it was less usual then for women to go to funerals. Before the funeral Cassandra wrote to Fanny a full account of the deathbed, opening her letter – 'My dearest Fanny – doubly dear to me now for her dear sake whom we have lost' – and told her that as Jane Austen lay in her coffin, 'there is such a sweet serene air over her countenance as is quite pleasant to contemplate.' After the funeral she wrote to Fanny again:

> Thursday was not so dreadful a day to me as you imagined. There was so much necessary to be done that there was no time for additional misery. Everything was conducted with the greatest tranquillity, and but that I was determined I would see the last, and therefore was upon the listen, I should not have known when they left the house. I watched the little mournful procession the length of the street; and when it turned from my sight, and I had lost her for ever, even then I was not overpowered, nor so much agitated as I am now in writing of it. Never was human being more sincerely mourned by those who attended her remains than was this dear creature.

Henry Austen undertook the task of seeing his sister's last work through the press. Prefaced with a 'Biographical Notice of the Author' by himself, *Northanger Abbey* and *Persuasion* appeared together in December 1817 (the date on the title-page was 1818) in four volumes at 24s., the edition being of 2,500 copies. The title *Northanger Abbey* was given by Henry.

'Northanger Abbey' and 'Persuasion' Published

What happened next? Jane Austen would have sympathized with a wish to know what became of the family to whom she was devoted.

James Austen died in 1819. Henry came over to care for Steventon parish until in 1823 his nephew William Knight, who had ridden by Jane Austen's carriage when she went to Winchester, was ready to take charge. Henry then went back to Bentley and became Perpetual Curate there. He made a second marriage in 1820 to Eleanor Jackson, a niece of Rev. John Papillon, the Rector of Chawton, whom Jane Austen had laughingly spoken of marrying. Eventually he retired to France and then to Tonbridge, his father's first home, and died there in 1850. Edward Knight lived at Chawton till his death in 1852; there are Knights at Chawton still. Francis Austen's first wife, Mary, died in 1823, and in 1828 he

Admiral Sir Francis Austen

married Martha Lloyd, who thus became Mrs Austen's daughter-in-law after all; he received a K.C.B. in 1837, became an Admiral of the Fleet and lived until 1865. Charles, the youngest of the family, became an Admiral, and died in Burma in 1852.

For some time Mrs Austen and Cassandra lived on together at the Chawton cottage. 'Ah, my dear, I fear you find me just where you left me – on the sofa',

Rear-Admiral Charles Austen

said old Mrs Austen to Edward Austen-Leigh on one of his visits, 'I sometimes think that God Almighty must have forgotten me; but I dare say He will come for me in His own good time.' She died in 1827, at the age of 88. Cassandra died in 1845, at Francis Austen's house near Portsmouth.

None of the nephews and nieces of whom Jane Austen was especially fond became a novelist. Anna Lefroy destroyed her novel after her aunt's death, telling

Title-pages of the first
editions of Jane Austen's
major novels

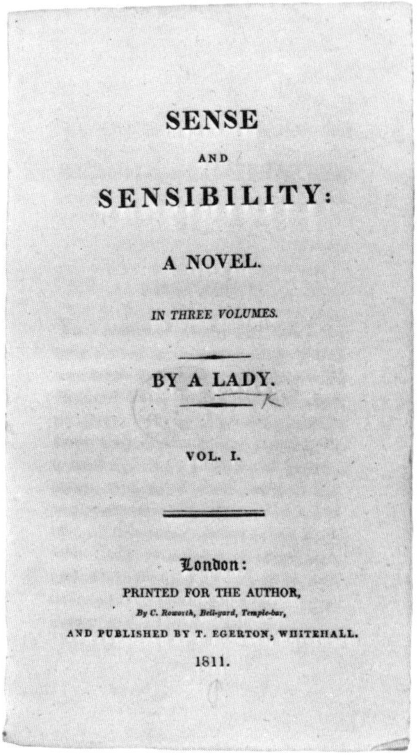

SENSE

AND

SENSIBILITY:

A NOVEL.

IN THREE VOLUMES.

BY A LADY.

VOL. I.

London:
PRINTED FOR THE AUTHOR,
By C. Roworth, Bell-yard, Temple-bar,
AND PUBLISHED BY T. EGERTON, WHITEHALL.
1811.

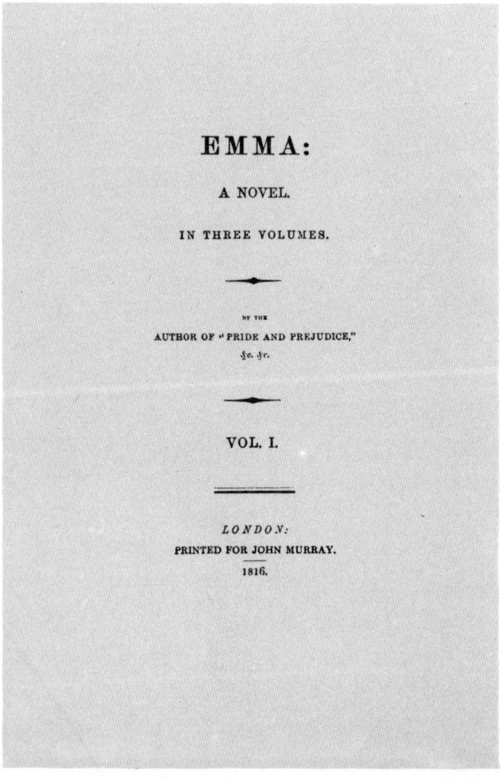

EMMA:

A NOVEL.

IN THREE VOLUMES.

BY THE
AUTHOR OF "PRIDE AND PREJUDICE,"
&c. &c.

VOL. I.

LONDON:
PRINTED FOR JOHN MURRAY.
1816.

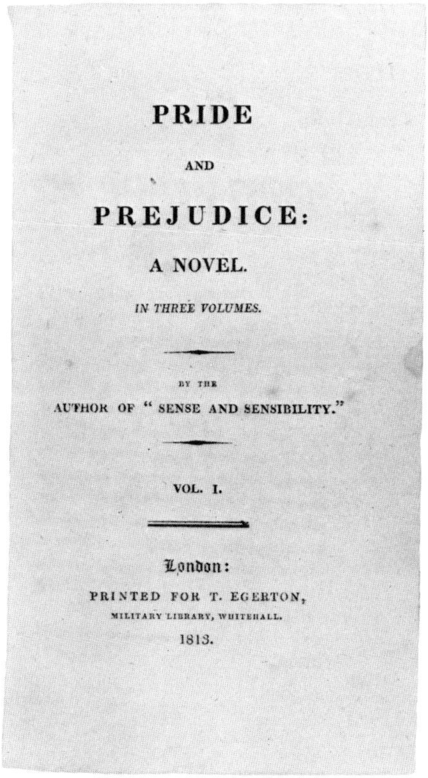

PRIDE

AND

PREJUDICE:

A NOVEL.

IN THREE VOLUMES.

————————

BY THE
AUTHOR OF " SENSE AND SENSIBILITY."

————————

VOL. I.

————————

London:
PRINTED FOR T. EGERTON,
MILITARY LIBRARY, WHITEHALL.
1813.

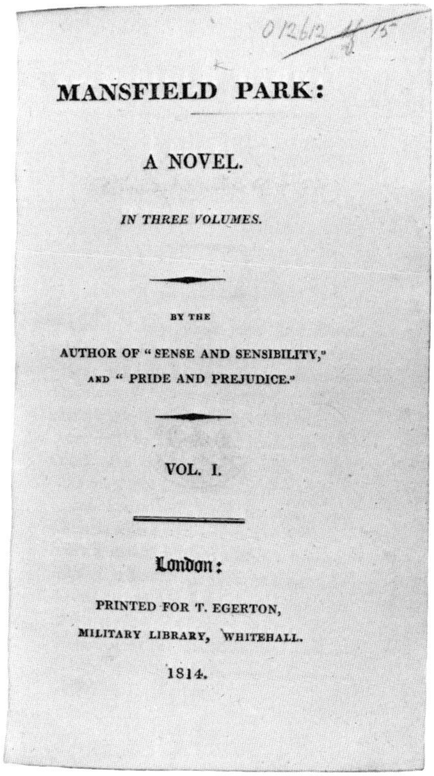

MANSFIELD PARK:

A NOVEL.

IN THREE VOLUMES.

————————

BY THE
AUTHOR OF " SENSE AND SENSIBILITY,"
AND " PRIDE AND PREJUDICE."

————————

VOL. I.

————————

London:
PRINTED FOR T. EGERTON,
MILITARY LIBRARY, WHITEHALL.
1814.

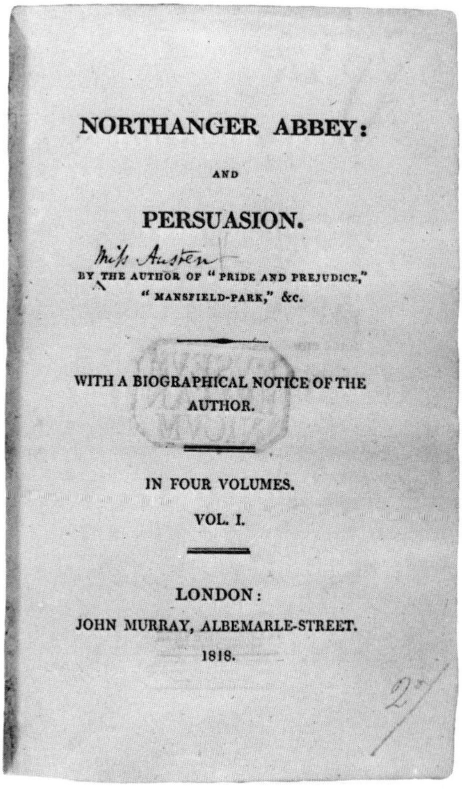

NORTHANGER ABBEY:

AND

PERSUASION.

Miss Austen

BY THE AUTHOR OF " PRIDE AND PREJUDICE,"
" MANSFIELD-PARK," &c.

————————

WITH A BIOGRAPHICAL NOTICE OF THE
AUTHOR.

————————

IN FOUR VOLUMES.
VOL. I.

————————

LONDON:
JOHN MURRAY, ALBEMARLE-STREET.
1818.

her daughter that she could not bear to go on with it, it reminded her so much of the loss of her aunt. Edward Austen-Leigh is of course best known for his Memoir of his aunt, but he also published in 1865 a pleasant book about the Steventon neighbourhood called *Recollections of the Early Days of the Vine Hunt*. To Caroline we owe the loving memories she wrote down in 1867.

And Fanny, 'dearest Fanny', Fanny who was the delight of her aunt's life, 'almost another Sister'? Fanny eventually made a 'good' marriage. In 1820, she married Sir Edward Knatchbull, Bt, and grew ashamed of her Austen relations. Cassandra had bequeathed Jane's letters to Fanny, but when Edward Austen-Leigh asked for them for his Memoir, she professed herself unable to find them. And where no other relation of Jane Austen's had ever, after her death, anything but good to recall of her, Fanny's recollections were, or became, quite other. In an undated letter to a younger sister she wrote,

> Yes my love it is very true that Aunt Jane for various circumstances was not so *refined* as she ought to have been for her *talent*, & if she had lived 50 years later she would have been in many ways more suitable to *our* more refined tastes. They were not rich & the people around with whom they chiefly mixed, were not at all high bred, or in short anything more than *mediocre* & *they* of course tho'

The Vine Hunt, the subject of Edward Austen-Leigh's first book

Lady Knatchbull, *née* Fanny Knight (Austen)

superior in *mental powers* & *cultivation* were on the same level as far as *refinement* goes – but I think in later life their intercourse with Mrs. Knight (who was very fond of & kind to them) improved them both & Aunt Jane was too clever not to put aside all possible signs of 'common⁄ness' (if such an expression is allowable) & teach herself to be more refined, at least in intercourse with people in general. Both the Aunts (Cass. & Jane) were brought up in the most com⁄plete ignorance of the World & its ways (I mean as to fashion, &c) & if it had not been for Papa's marriage which brought them into Kent, & the kindness of Mrs. Knight who used often to have one or the other of the sisters staying with her, they would have been, tho' not less clever & agreeable in themselves, very much below par as to good Society and its ways. If you hate all this I beg yr. pardon, but I felt it at my *pen's end*, & it chose to come along & speak the truth. It is now nearly dressing time –

Had the writer been anyone but her dearest Fanny, it is a letter that would surely have been enjoyed by Jane Austen.

The nave of Winchester Cathedral ▶

1775 16 December Jane Austen born at Steventon.

1782–(?)87 Jane and Cassandra at school at Oxford, Southampton and Reading.

c. 1786–87 Amateur theatricals at Steventon. Jane begins to write.

By 1793 *Volume the First, Volume the Second* and *Volume the Third* completed and fair-copied.

1794 *Elinor and Marianne* started. Mrs Radcliffe's *Mysteries of Udolpho* published.

1795–96 Love affair with Tom Lefroy.

1796 9 January Jane's surviving letters begin. *Elinor and Marianne* completed. *First Impressions* started. Fanny Burney's *Camilla* published.

1797 *First Impressions* offered for publication without effect. *Sense and Sensibility* (the former *Elinor and Marianne*) started.

1798 Samuel Blackall makes tentative amatory approaches. (?) *Susan* written.

c. 1799 Jane writing *Lady Susan*.

1800 Jane's father decides to retire.

1801 Mr and Mrs Austen, with Cassandra and Jane, move to Bath. Visit to Sidmouth; (?) Jane's love affair with a clergyman.

1802 Harris Bigg-Wither proposes to Jane.

1803 *Susan* sold to Crosby & Co. but not published. (?) *The Watsons* begun.

1804 Visit to Lyme.

1805 Mr Austen dies at Bath. Jane makes fair copy of *Lady Susan* and abandons *The Watsons*.

1806 Mrs Austen, Cassandra and Jane leave Bath and settle at Southampton with Martha Lloyd and Frank Austen and his wife.

1809 Mrs Austen, Cassandra, Jane and Martha Lloyd move to Chawton.

1811 *Mansfield Park* started. November Publication of *Sense and Sensibility*.

1813 January Publication of *Pride and Prejudice* (the revised *First Impressions*). *Mansfield Park* completed. Second impressions of *Sense and Sensibility* and *Pride and Prejudice*.

1814 May *Mansfield Park* published. *Emma* started.

1815 Jane invited to dedicate her next novel to the Prince Regent.
Emma completed, *Persuasion* begun.
Susan bought back from Crosby & Co.
Publication of *Raison et Sensibilité,* first foreign translation.
December   *Emma* published.

1816 *Persuasion* completed, *Susan* revised.
Second impression of *Mansfield Park.*

Publication of *Le Parc de Mansfield* and *La Nouvelle Emma.*
Jane's health begins to fail.

1817 *Sanditon* begun.
24 May   Jane and Cassandra move to lodgings in Winchester.
18 July   Jane Austen dies.
December   Publication of *Northanger Abbey* (the revised *Susan*) and *Persuasion* in one volume dated 1818.

5 MAP of northern Hampshire; from W. Tunncliffe, *A Topographical Survey of the Western Circuit*, 1791.

7 THOMAS MACAULAY; portrait by F. Grant. Macaulay wrote in his *Essay on Madame d'Arblay*, 'Shakespeare has had neither equal nor second. But among the writers who . . . have approached nearest to the manner of the great master, we have no hesitation in placing Jane Austen.' *National Portrait Gallery, London*

ALFRED LORD TENNYSON; bust by T. Woolner. According to an undated letter from Mrs Cameron, 'Alfred talked very pleasantly that evening to Annie Thackeray and L–S–. He spoke of Jane Austen, as James Spedding does, as next to Shake-speare!' *Westminster Abbey, London*

THE REV. GEORGE AUSTEN; anonymous miniature. Jane Austen House, Chawton. *Photo J. Butler-Kearney*

FRANCIS AUSTEN of Sevenoaks; portrait by O. Humphrey. *Sheffield City Art Galleries*

8 TONBRIDGE SCHOOL as it looked from 1760 to 1825; from S. Rivington, *The History of Tonbridge School*, 1869.

WALCOT CHURCH, Bath; pen and ink drawing by S. H. Grimm, 1790. From the Kaye Collection. *Courtesy the Trustees of the British Museum*

9 'TASTE, or Burlington Gate'; engraving by W. Hogarth, December–January 1731/32. Pope's epistle, which satirized the Duke of Chandos, was, on its first publication in 1731, entitled 'Of Taste: an Epistle to the Rt. Honble. Richard, Earl of Burlington, occasioned by his publishing "Palladio's Designs" etc.'; it was afterwards called 'Of False Taste' and, finally, as Epistle IV of the *Moral Essays*, 'Of the Use of Riches'.

10 ASHE RECTORY; from M. C. Hill, *Jane Austen. Her homes and her friends*, 1902.

DEANE HOUSE; from M. C. Hill, *Jane Austen. Her homes and her friends*, 1902.

11 STEVENTON RECTORY; drawing by Anna Lefroy. Jane Austen House, Chawton. *Photo J. Butler-Kearney*

12–13 GODMERSHAM PARK, Kent; from E. Hasted, *The History and Topographical Survey of the County of Kent*, 1799. By the time this picture was published, Thomas Knight had died (1794) and his widow had made over the property to Edward Austen.

THE COUNTRYSIDE near Selborne; from G. White, *The Natural History and Anti-quities of Selborne*, 1789. Gilbert White's Selborne was a little to the south of Alton. John White of Selborne, nephew of the naturalist, and his family were friends of the Austens. *Photo courtesy Ruth Rosenberg*

131

Notes 15 THE REV. JAMES AUSTEN; from M.C. Hill, *Jane Austen. Her homes and her friends*, 1902.

MRS GEORGE AUSTEN; from M.C. Hill, *Jane Austen. Her homes and her friends*, 1902.

16 COACH AND HORSES; drawing by P. Sandby, *c.* 1750. Royal Library, Windsor. *Reproduced by Gracious Permission of Her Majesty the Queen*

17 MRS PHILADELPHIA HANCOCK; after a miniature by J. Smart. Jane Austen House, Chawton. *Photo J. Butler-Kearney*

18–19 THE TRIAL of Warren Hastings, 13 February 1788. Engraved by R. Pollard and aquatinted by F. Jukes after E. Dayes. *Courtesy the Trustees of the British Museum*

19 HURSTBOURNE PARK; from R. Mudie, *Hampshire*, 1838.

20 THE REV. GEORGE AUSTEN presenting his son Edward to Mr and Mrs Thomas Knight; silhouette, *c.* 1778. Jane Austen House, Chawton. *Photo J. Butler-Kearney*

THOMAS KNIGHT; portrait by George Romney. *By kind permission of Brigadier B.C. Bradford*

CATHERINE KNIGHT; portrait by George Romney. *By kind permission of Brigadier B.C. Bradford*

21 LIBERALITY to infirm beggars on leaving Yvri; from *Repository of Arts*, Jan. 1817.

MUSÉE des Monuments Français, Paris; painting by Hubert Robert, *c.* 1800. *Kunsthalle, Bremen*

22 ST JOHN'S COLLEGE, Oxford, from the garden; engraving by M. Rooker, 1783. British Museum. *Photo R.B. Fleming*

23 THE REV. HENRY AUSTEN; anonymous portrait: Jane Austen House, Chawton. *Photo J. Butler-Kearney*

24 THE GATEWAY of the Old Abbey, Reading; engraving by P. Sandby. *Photo Courtauld Institute of Art*

25 ILLUSTRATION to Goethe's *Die Leiden des jungen Werthers*, by D. Chodowiecki, 1775.

TITLE-PAGE of Oliver Goldsmith's *An History of England*, 1764.

26–27 ROYAL NAVAL ACADEMY, Portsmouth; lithograph by J.T. Lee, 1806. *Plymouth City Museums (Southsea Castle)*

28 MADAME DE FEUILLIDE; from M.C. Hill, *Jane Austen. Her homes and her friends*, 1902.

SCENE from David Garrick's *Bon Ton*; engraved for J. Powell, 1793. Endhoven Collection. *Victoria and Albert Museum.*

28–29 BRANDENBURG HOUSE THEATRE, Hammersmith; drawing by H. Wigstead, *c.* 1792–93. *From the collection of Mr and Mrs Paul Mellon*

31 ILLUSTRATION to J.-J. Rousseau's *La Nouvelle Héloïse*; India ink, wash and pen drawing by F. Wheatley, 1786. *Courtesy the Trustees of the British Museum*

32 ANGEL INN, Basingstoke; trade card. *Hampshire County Museum Service*

MANYDOWN HOUSE; from G.F. Prosser, *Select Illustrations of Hampshire*, 1833.

33 SCORE of the 'Boulanger' music. Jane Austen House, Chawton. *Photo J. Butler-Kearney*

THE SQUIRE'S CONVALESCENCE; anonymous painting, early nineteenth century. *The Beaverbrook Foundations*

35 THE REV. ISAAC LEFROY; miniature. Jane Austen House, Chawton. *Photo J. Butler-Kearney*

Sir Egerton Brydges; from his *Autobiography*, 1834.

Mary Russell Mitford, aged three; from *The Lady's Companion*, July 1852.

36 OVERTON; from R. Mudie, *Hampshire*, 1838.

37 EDWARD (AUSTEN) KNIGHT, aged 21; anonymous portrait painted in 1789 during the Grand Tour. By kind permission of Alton Urban District council. *Photo J. Butler-Kearney*

ELIZABETH AUSTEN (née Bridges); miniature by R. Cosway. Jane Austen House, Chawton. *Photo J. Butler-Kearney*

38 A CAPTAIN'S UNIFORM in the Oxford Militia; watercolour *c.* 1800. Jane Austen House, Chawton. *Photo J. Butler-Kearney*

COMMEMORATION of the taking of the Bastille in 1792; from *Tableaux historiques de la Révolution Français*, 1804.

39 THE ENGLISH FRIGATE 'Unicorn' and the French frigate 'La Tribune', 8 June 1796; from M.C. Hill, *Jane Austen. Her homes and her friends*, 1902.

40-41 WELBECK, a garden designed by H. Repton; from Repton's *Sketches and Hints on Landscape Gardening*, 1794.

41 CASSANDRA ELIZABETH AUSTEN; silhouette. Jane Austen House, Chawton. *Photo J. Butler-Kearney*

42 James Leigh Perrot; silhouette. Jane Austen House, Chawton. *Photo J. Butler-Kearney*

42-43 AXFORD AND PARAGON BUILDINGS, Bath; from J.G. Nattes, *Bath*, 1806.

43 MRS LEIGH PERROT; silhouette. Jane Austen House, Chawton. *Photo J. Butler-Kearney*

PUMP OF THE KING'S BATH, Bath, 1788. 'Edward drinks at the Hetling Pump, is to bathe tomorrow, & try Electricity on Tuesday . . . we are all unanimous in expecting no advantage of it.' (*Letter* from JA to Cassandra, 2 June 1799). From the Kaye Collection. *Courtesy the Trustees of the British Museum*

44 ACCOUNT of Mrs Leigh Perrot's trial; from *The Lady's Magazine*, April 1800.

45 THOMAS LEFROY; miniature by G. Engleheart, 1799. *By kind permission of Miss Phoebe Lefroy*

47 FELLOW COMMONER of Emmanuel, Nobleman and Fellow Commoner of Trinity, Cambridge; watercolour by T. Uwins, 1815. *Courtesy the Trustees of the British Museum*

BAYE DE JACQUEMEL, Santo Domingo; engraving by N. Ponce. British Museum. *Photo R.B. Fleming*

49 PORTMAN SQUARE; watercolour drawing by Gingal. British Museum

50-51 THE CIRCULATING LIBRARY in Milsom Street, Bath; anonymous engraving, 1829. *Photo Courtauld Institute of Art*

51 FANNY BURNEY; portrait by E. Burney. *National Portrait Gallery, London*

51 ILLUSTRATION from Mrs Radcliffe's *Mysteries of Udolpho*, 1803.

53 MORNING DRESS; from N. Heideloff, *Gallery of Fashion*, October 1801.

SYDNEY GARDENS, Bath; from J. G. Nattes, *Bath*, 1806.

54 TEIGNMOUTH; engraving by W. Spreat. *Courtesy the Trustees of the British Museum*

55 THE STRAND, Dawlish; engraving by G. Townsend. *Courtesy the Trustees of the British Museum*

'THE BATHING PLACE at Ramsgate'; painting by Benjamin West, 1780. *From the collection of Mr and Mrs Paul Mellon*

56–57 THE NEW ASSEMBLY ROOMS, Bath; from J. G. Nattes, *Bath*, 1806.

58 VIEW OF DORKING; from T. Allen, *History of Surrey*, 1831.

58–59 VIEW OF LYME REGIS; anonymous watercolour. *Courtesy the Trustees of the British Museum*

59 'VIEW FROM POLSDEN near Bookham'; watercolour drawing by J. Varley, 1800. It was near here that Madame d'Arblay lived; and at Bookham Mrs Austen's cousins, the Samuel Cookes. 'I shall be nearer to Bookham than I c^d wish, in going from Dorking to Guildford.' (*Letter* from JA to Cassandra, 26 June 1808) *Laing Art Gallery, Newcastle upon Tyne*

60 THE PUMP ROOM, Bath; from R. Warner, *The History of Bath*, 1801.

61 'CLIFTON ROCKS from Rownham Fields'; painting by F. Danby, *c.* 1820. 'We shall drive directly to Clifton and dine there.' (*Northanger Abbey*, Ch. XI, Vol. I.) *City Art Gallery, Bristol. On loan to the Tate Gallery, London*

62–63 'THE CLOAKROOM, Clifton Assembly Rooms'; painting by R. Sharples, 1817–18. *City Art Gallery, Bristol*

64 'L'AIMABLE JANE'; silhouette thought to represent Jane Austen. *National Portrait Gallery, London*

65 STONELEIGH ABBEY; from W. Smith, *A new and compendious History of Warwick*, 1830.

CASTLE SQUARE, Southampton; anonymous engraving. The garden of 2 Castle Square led down to the ramparts between these two towers. Jane Austen House, Chawton. *Photo J. Butler-Kearney*

66 HOUSES IN ST MICHAEL'S PLACE, London; from T. C. Croker, *A Walk from London to Fulham*, 1896.

66–67 WINCHESTER COLLEGE; anonymous drawing. *Courtauld Institute of Art*

67 LADIES TAKING AN AIRING in a phaeton; from N. Heideloff, *Gallery of Fashion*, August 1794.

68–69 SIR JOHN MOORE and his troops crossing the Tagus near Villa Velha during the Peninsular War; from W. Bradford, *Sketches of Country, Character and Costume in Portugal and Spain made during the Campaign and on the route of the British Army in 1808 and 1809*. 'This is grievous news from Spain. – It is well that Dr. Moore was spared the knowledge of such a son's death.' (*Letter* from JA to Cassandra, 24 January 1809)

70 CHAWTON COTTAGE. *Copyright Country Life*

71 JANE AUSTEN; pen and watercolour portrait by her sister Cassandra, *c.* 1810. *National Portrait Gallery, London*

72 THE HIGH STREET, Alton; engraving by Newman. *Curtis Museum, Alton*

72–73 CHAWTON HOUSE in Jane Austen's time; anonymous gouache. *Copyright Country Life*

74 JANE AUSTEN'S MUSIC BOOKS. Jane Austen House, Chawton. *Photo J. Butler-Kearney*

75 COLLIER'S LONDON to Winchester Coach; anonymous watercolour, *c.* 1800. *Curtis Museum, Alton*

76 DETAIL OF QUILT made by Jane Austen, Cassandra and Mrs Austen. Jane Austen House, Chawton. *Photo J. Butler-Kearney*

77 PORTRAIT OF JANE AUSTEN from the 1870 Memoir by Edward Austen-Leigh; engraving, presumably from Cassandra's sketch portrait (p. 71). Jane Austen House, Chawton. *Photo J. Butler-Kearney*

79 FANNY CATHERINE AUSTEN; pencil portrait by Jane Austen. Jane Austen House, Chawton. *Photo J. Butler-Kearney*

80–81 MESSRS HARDING, HOWELL & CO., Pall Mall; from *Repository of Arts*, 1800. ' – in a Linendraper's shop . . . I was tempted by a pretty coloured muslin, and bought 10 y^{ds} of it, on the chance of your liking it.' (*Letter* from JA to Cassandra, 18 April 1811)

WEDGWOOD AND BYERLEY, York Street, St James's Square; from *Repository of Arts*, 1800.

81 'MRS SIDDONS AS LADY MACBETH seizing the daggers'; painting by H. Fuseli exhibited in 1812. *Tate Gallery, London*

82–83 'STREATHAM COMMON'; watercolour by P. de Wint. *Private collection*

Notes

83 VIEW OF WHITEHALL from Parliament Street; engraving by R. Rosse after G. Shepherd, 1810. British Museum. *Photo R.B. Fleming*

84 MRS LEIGH PERROT; from *The Lady's Magazine*, April 1800.

85 MRS BENNET and her two youngest daughters; illustration by Hugh Thompson in the George Allen edition (1894) of *Pride and Prejudice.*

86 WARREN HASTINGS; portrait by Sir Thomas Lawrence, 1811. *National Portrait Gallery, London*

87 SIR WALTER SCOTT; portrait by Edwin Landseer, 1824. *National Portrait Gallery, London*

88–89 SPRING GARDENS, London; watercolour by T. Shepherd. *Courtesy the Trustees of the British Museum.*

89 AN EXHIBITION of watercolour drawings; from T. Rowlandson and A. Pugin, *Microcosm of London*, 1808.

90 THE REV. BENJAMIN LEFROY; after a miniature by R. Ubsdell. Jane Austen House, Chawton. *Photo J. Butler-Kearney*

91 HENRIETTA STREET, Covent Garden; drawing by T. Dibdin. *Guildhall Library, London*

92–93 'SEIZED UP IN THE RIGGING'; from A. Burton, *The Adventures of Johnny Newcombe in the Navy*, 1818.

93 ILLUSTRATION by Hugh Thompson for the Macmillan edition (1897) of *Persuasion.*

95 'SLEEPY CONGREGATION'; engraving by T. Rowlandson, 1811. *Courtesy the Trustees of the British Museum*

SCENE from 'The Clandestine Marriage'; painting by John Zoffany, *c.* 1769. Garrick's play was first produced in 1766; this scene so pleased George III and Queen Charlotte that they commissioned Zoffany to paint this picture. *By kind permission of the Garrick Club, London*

96 ANNA LEFROY; after a miniature by R. Ubsdell. Jane Austen House, Chawton. *Photo J. Butler-Kearney*

97 CAPTAIN CHARLES AUSTEN; anonymous portrait. Jane Austen House, Chawton. *Photo J. Butler-Kearney*

98 HOUSE IN HANS PLACE; from T.C. Croker, *A Walk from London to Fulham*, 1860.

THE MEETING of Byron and Scott at John Murray's in 1815; painting by L. Werner, *c.* 1850. *In the possession of John Murray*

99 A COMMON ARMENIACA APRICOT; from H.L. Duhamel du Monceau, *Traité des arbres fruitiers*, 1768.

100–101 'THE PRINCE REGENT driving Mrs Q on the road to Brighton'; engraving by T. Rowlandson. *Photo Courtauld Institute of Art*

101 THE PRINCE REGENT'S copy of 'Emma'. ' – it is my particular wish that one Set should be completed & sent to H.R.H. two or three days before the Work is generally public.' (*Letter* from JA to John Murray, 11 December 1815) Royal Library, Windsor. *Reproduced by Gracious Permission of Her Majesty the Queen*

102–103 THE CRIMSON DRAWING-ROOM, Carlton House; from W.H. Pyne, *The History of the Royal Residences*, 1819. '–the many flattering attentions which I rec^d from you at Carlton House on Monday last.' (*Letter* from JA to the Rev. James Stainer Clarke, 15 November 1815)

104 PRINCESS CHARLOTTE; portrait by G. Dawe. *National Portrait Gallery, London*

PRINCE LEOPOLD of Saxe-Coburg-Saalfeld; engraving after E. Chalon in *Repository of Arts*, July 1816. He was later King of the Belgians, and Queen Victoria's 'Uncle Leopold'.

105 MARIA EDGEWORTH; from E.A. Duyckinck, *Portrait Gallery of Eminent Women*, 1813.

106 BOX HILL AND BURFORD; from F. Shoberl, *Topography of Surrey*, 1868.

107 LEATHERHEAD CHURCH; from W.E. Trotter, *Select Illustrated Topography*, 1839.

109 WYARDS, home of Ben and Anna Lefroy; anonymous painting, *c.* 1800. Jane Austen House, Chawton. *Photo J. Butler-Kearney*

110 THE VILLAGE GREEN, Bentley. *Curtis Museum, Alton*

111 THE OPENING of Ch. X of 'Persuasion', later rewritten; 1 July 1803. *Courtesy the Trustees of the British Museum*

112–113 THE OLD WELLS and Pump Room, Cheltenham; engraving by H. Merke after T. Hulley, 1813. British Museum. *Photo R.B. Fleming*

115 MR WILLIAM CURTIS, apothecary at Alton; anonymous portrait. *Curtis Museum, Alton*

116–117 THE HIGH STREET, Winchester; from R. Mudie, *Hampshire*, 1838.

118 NO. 8 COLLEGE STREET, Winchester, the house in which Jane Austen died. *Photo J. Butler-Kearney*

120 THE ROOM in which Jane Austen died. *Photo J. Butler-Kearney*

122 ADMIRAL SIR FRANCIS AUSTEN; anonymous portrait. Jane Austen House, Chawton. *Photo J. Butler-Kearney*

123 REAR-ADMIRAL CHARLES AUSTEN; anonymous portrait. Jane Austen House, Chawton. *Photo J. Butler-Kearney*

124 TITLE-PAGE of 'Sense and Sensibility', 1811.

TITLE-PAGE of 'Emma', 1816.

125 TITLE-PAGE of 'Pride and Prejudice', *Notes* 1813.

TITLE-PAGE of 'Mansfield Park', 1814.

TITLE-PAGE of 'Northanger Abbey' and 'Persuasion', 1818.

126 'THE VINE HUNT'; engraving by H. Calvert, 1844. The picture shows a scene in Hurstbourne Park, with the Duke of Wellington and his daughter-in-law at upper right. Hampshire County Museum Service. *Photo D. R. Stephens*

127 LADY KNATCHBULL (Fanny Knight); anonymous portrait. Jane Austen House, Chawton. *Photo J. Butler-Kearney*

128 THE NAVE of Winchester Cathedral; from J. Britton, *The History and Antiquities of the See and Cathedral of Winchester*, 1817.

SELECT BIBLIOGRAPHY

I WORKS BY JANE AUSTEN

a *The major novels*
These, with their dates of first publication, are:

1811 *Sense and Sensibility*
1813 *Pride and Prejudice*
1814 *Mansfield Park*
1816 *Emma*
1818 *Northanger Abbey* and *Persuasion*

Several editions of the novels are available. The definitive edition, with full critical apparatus, is that edited by R. W. Chapman and published by the Oxford University Press.

b *The minor works*
A full collection of the minor works is to be found in Volume VI of R. W. Chapman's edition of the novels. This includes the Juvenilia *(Volume the First, Volume the Second* in which is *Love and Freindship* and *The History of England,* and *Volume the Third);* the short early novel *Lady Susan (c.* 1805); the two fragments of novels, *The Watsons (c.* 1803) and *Sanditon* (1817); the *Plan of a Novel (c.* 1815); *Opinions of 'Mansfield Park' and 'Emma' (c.* 1816), and verses and prayers.

Charades by Jane Austen and her family were printed in *Personal Aspects* (see *General Works,* below).

The cancelled chapter of *Persuasion* is to be found in R. W. Chapman's edition of *Persuasion.*

c *The Letters*
The definitive edition is that of R. W. Chapman (2nd edition, 1952).

II GENERAL WORKS

This lists only those works principally consulted in the preparation of this book.

1867 Caroline Austen. *My Aunt Jane Austen* (printed for the Jane Austen Society, 1952)

1870 J.E. Austen-Leigh. *A Memoir of Jane Austen*
1902 Constance Hill. *Jane Austen. Her homes and her friends*
1906 John H. and Edith Hubback. *Jane Austen's Sailor Brothers*
1913 William and Richard Arthur Austen-Leigh. *Jane Austen, Her Life and Letters, a Family Record*
1920 Mary Augusta Austen-Leigh. *Personal Aspects of Jane Austen*
1929 C. Linklater Thomson. *Jane Austen, a Survey*
1938 Elizabeth Jenkins. *Jane Austen, a Biography*
1939 Mary Lascelles. *Jane Austen and her Art*
1948 R.W. Chapman. *Jane Austen, Facts and Problems*
1953 R.W. Chapman. *Jane Austen, a Critical Biography*
1964 B.C. Southam. *Jane Austen's Literary Manuscripts*
1967 *Collected Reports of the Jane Austen Society, 1949–1965*
1968 B.C. Southam. *Jane Austen, the Critical Heritage*

The undated letter from Lady Knatchbull (Fanny Knight) on pp. 126–27 was printed in the *Cornhill* no. 973, Winter 1947–48.

The letter by Maria Edgeworth, quoted on pp. 105–06, was first published in the *Times Literary Supplement* on 29 February 1968.

INDEX

Page numbers in italics refer to illustrations.
Jane Austen herself, her parents and her brothers and sister, appearing passim *throughout,*
are only indexed where they are the subjects of illustrations